# A Year on Our Farm

# A Year on Our Farm

*How The Countryside Made Me*

MATT BAKER

MICHAEL  JOSEPH

MICHAEL JOSEPH

UK | USA | Canada | Ireland | Australia
India | New Zealand | South Africa

Michael Joseph is part of the Penguin Random House group of companies
whose addresses can be found at global.penguinrandomhouse.com

Penguin
Random House
UK

First published 2021

**006**

Copyright © Matt Baker, 2021

The moral right of the author has been asserted

Set in 14 /17 pt Garamond

Typeset by Couper Street Type Co.

Printed and bound in Great Britain by Clays Ltd, Elcograf S.p.A.

A CIP catalogue record for this book is available from the British Library

ISBN: 978–0–241–54273–6

www.greenpenguin.co.uk

# Contents

# Introduction

## Behind the Farm Gate

Welcome to our farm in the Dales!

A one-hundred-acre organic sheep farm, perched on the side of a valley in the Durham hills, with an ancient woodland, heritage-breed sheep, miniature donkeys, goats, sheepdogs, chickens and the most beautiful views anyone could wish for.

No matter what is going on in my life, no matter what direction my career is taking me in, no matter what kind of successes or challenges I am faced with, the farm has always been a constant part of my life. It has helped me to put – and keep – everything in perspective.

The farm has made me who I am and it always *reminds* me of who I am.

In general, people are quite surprised that there is more to me than the guy who was always sitting on a green sofa at seven o'clock talking to other people about what they were up to in their lives. I love hearing stories; I love talking to people; I love being around individuals who have experiences and opinions and tales to tell. As the person doing the interviews, there was never really an onus on me to say what I was up to, or what was happening in my life. You may know me from *Countryfile*, *The One Show* or, earlier than that, *Blue Peter*, but I had a life before any of those shows, at the top of my sport in Britain, and I have certainly had many memorable moments outside of that TV world before and since. I have been so fortunate to travel the globe meeting people from every walk of life, from famous faces to solitary, remote nomads who live two days' walk from the nearest village. I've filled three passports with those adventures and over many years these experiences have really helped me to understand what is important in my life and motivated me to focus on what I believe in.

Yet there is one destination that I will always choose above all others.

The farm, with my family.

After every adventure and memorable experience overseas or on these shores, I always come back to the farm, living the life that I love, with these animals, in these fields, in this valley.

You know when you've been away on holiday and you're flying home? You take off and the landscape falls away beneath you as the plane disappears into the clouds. Then, as you start the descent back into the UK, you begin to see this green island from above and, as you get lower down, you can make out tree-tops, individual fields, maybe even some hedgerows or livestock . . .

When I see all that, I get this intensely reassuring feeling of *being home.*

That is exactly how the farm makes me feel every time I am here.

I love nothing more than driving up the farm track, closing the gate, shutting the world out . . . and just being here.

I love it.

I started writing this book the day after the very first episode of my TV show, *Our Farm in the Dales*, aired. That programme was about our farm, the place where I grew up, my family and our way of life. It was the most personal project I have ever been involved in – I produced and directed it, plus it involved my family for the first time.

Filming that show crystallized what is really important in my life: family, the farm, being in tune with nature, working hard and aiming high, enjoying what life has to offer but also seeing the beauty in the small things around us . . . above all, being so very grateful for growing up in a stunning landscape, surrounded by the incredible beauty of nature, right here, on my doorstep.

I am dyslexic, so I see the world very visually and, as a result, one of my hobbies is to draw. Scattered throughout these pages are some of my sketches from around the farm: animals, plants, ideas and scribblings, just stuff that inspires me. I love nothing more than taking a sketch pad down into the woods or across the valley and sitting down, surrounded by nature . . . just drawing or painting.

So settle in for a tour of our farm, taking in each of the four seasons in turn and detailing what happens, when and how, during those very different but equally remarkable phases of the farming year. Along the way I will tell you some of the adventures I've had away from the farm, somersaulting my way to a British championship, phoning the BBC switchboard after a phone call from my wife's aunty, jumping on to a sofa every weeknight in front of the nation for nine years, cycling a rickshaw for more miles than you can imagine, travelling the globe and meeting cowboys, tribespeople, film stars and fellow farmers.

With any luck, through the pages of this book, I can tell you a few of my stories, share some of the incredible experiences I've been fortunate enough to enjoy and, hopefully, give you an idea of what makes me tick.

I

# The Track to Baker's Acres

For the early years of my childhood, I lived in Easington village, County Durham, having been born there the day before Christmas Eve, 1977. Back then, we lived on a lovely smallholding and my dad ran a local newsagent's in Easington Colliery. A smallholding is basically a compact version of a farm, so we had goats there, we had horses, we had all sorts of different animals and other bits and pieces. A set-up like that is more about people who want to be self-sufficient, tending vegetable patches, looking after animals and so on, rather than those who are looking to make a commercial living from the land. Dad had his newsagent's while Mum looked after our family and all the animals as well as helping Dad in the shop.

It was a friendly village and I have happy memories of my early years there. Easington Village School was a lovely village primary school; my sister went there as well. It benefited from very small classes; in fact there were two years in each classroom. The school had a lot of really good art teachers, such as one lady that I had in my final year called Mrs Robinson. She used to paint all sorts of wonderful landscapes around the hallways of the corridors, and I would always get lost in her artwork on the way to my class. That's a habit that would return to me many years later . . . but I will come back to that . . .

Even as a young lad, I used to know everyone in the local area: all the farmers, my school friends and teachers; in fact, when I look back at my child-hood, the overriding memory is one of *community*. We existed as a community, provided for one another, looked out for each other, grew up together, and there were some fantastic characters that you came across, learned from, laughed with and spent time being around.

There were always a lot of conversations between local people, regardless of who was in the room, adults or children. The adults never spoke to the children in a patronizing or demeaning way; I never felt like a kid being spoken to by an adult, they were just all my friends and people I loved being around. I definitely think that helped me in later years when I ended up on the TV chatting away with anyone and everyone. Without even realizing it, I was learning the art of talking to people and finding out what makes them tick. There are so many people in the north-east that are just fantastic at talking with you; these are some of the greatest interviewers on the planet, but you won't see them anywhere near a television studio. They are usually to be found just chatting on a bus or in a pub. I learned more from them than you would from any media course.

There was a chap called Old Joe who used to live next door to us. Around the back of his place, he had these incredible tile mosaics of all kinds of birds on the walls on the outside of his building. I was too young to know what species they were exactly, but to me these mosaics were amazing, I absolutely loved them. He had a garage full of all his old motorbikes and there was a stove in there as well, at the back, so I used to go and look at the motorbikes, or sit in there and chat to him for hours by the warmth of the flames.

I was forever running round the fields, jumping over walls, clambering up trees, grappling with any-thing and bouncing around. Eventually, my mum and dad were like, 'Right! What are we going to do with him?!' They needed to find an outlet for all that energy and physicality . . . and quick!

When I was around the age of six, Mum came up with the idea of gymnastics, so off I went to the local leisure centre to try it out and see if I liked this sport. I remember that very first night as if it was yesterday. It was at a place called Seaham Leisure Centre. I remember how echoey the gym was when I walked in, and the distinctive sound of the crash mats – when you land on one, they sort of lift up and then drop back down again on the gym floor with this slapping sound. I could hear all the gym-nasts running down the vault runway and the noise of backflips, cartwheels, somersaults: just this busy, energetic gymnasium and such a distinctive sound.

I was the only boy there. At the start of the session they drafted me straight into the warm-up. The girls were all wearing these maroon hooded tops with a pink inner, which was the local club colours; I ended up having to get an outfit made in those colours to match, because they didn't have a version for boys. I had these white shorts on that felt like a cross between cardboard and tracing paper, they were so restrictive, so not exactly ideal!

Despite my 'cardboard' shorts, I was addicted to gymnastics straight away.

I had the best time that night and, suddenly, I was completely obsessed. Gymnastics was a natural fit for me. The only part of every training session that I didn't like was when my mum left, for no other reason than I missed her, and I was always really elated when she came back to pick me up.

The teacher there was called Mr Mullaney. He had this big moustache and looked a bit like the BBC presenter Des Lynam. He taught me all the foundations of great gymnastics, such as handstands, cartwheels and rolls. I found that I particularly loved being upside down – I think I spent more of my time upside down than I did the right way up when I was younger!

Most of all, I thrived on this feeling that I had found something I was really good at. A big part of this was because although I worked hard at school, it was a big struggle . . . because I am dyslexic. Back then, dyslexia wasn't really a 'thing'. At first, I didn't really understand why I found reading so difficult. I would look at the words on the page in my schoolbook and they would jump around or just look all jumbled up. Full stops and things like that are totally non-existent in my world: I don't know where one sentence ends and the next begins, because if you are like me, you are just looking at these long strings of words and sometimes sentences will even move on to different lines. You find yourself stopping mid-sentence, because you can't follow what you are seeing, then you restart and maybe manufacture your own ending to the sentence. So being in class could be a nightmare – especially if I was asked to read something out loud from a book. What I would do was try to guess where my turn would land in the text, so I'd count everyone reading out loud before me, then figure out how much they might get through and which section would be me – then I would read this part ahead of my turn, and try to memorize the words. Of course, most of the time, I wouldn't guess correctly or the teacher would change the page or chapter, and knowing this could happen used to make me so anxious. (In later years, I have come to have a totally different view of my dyslexia, which I will come back to later in this book.)

There are some really artistic and creative minds in my family. My sister is an unbelievable artist and a brilliant jeweller and, in fact, she's my main inspiration with art. I do know that ever since I was little,

I've LOVED sketching and drawing – I was always scribbling cartoons, whilst my sister would paint. For a while there, it was my dream to be a cartoonist and the idea of going to Disney World was the ultimate ambition.

Cartoons were a different matter to reading. No problems, only enjoyment. No issues with confidence, only fun. I was always doodling; I drew for hours and hours and hours. It was how I could communicate. Consequently, I grew up in a very visual world. It is a well-known neuroscientific fact that some people comprehend their experiences visually, while others may do so with words or even sounds. I am certainly one of the former – painting and drawing to me is no different to talking or writing, in terms of self-expression. I was also very energetic as a kid, so art was a way for me to sit down and rest, but it was *productive* rest. I couldn't sit still and just do nothing, I certainly couldn't sit down and read a book, and if I didn't want to go and watch telly, what was I doing? Well, for me, getting some colouring pencils out to draw anything was addictive. I would literally draw anywhere and everywhere, even on the back of a cereal packet if I couldn't find any paper to hand! I remember one drawing of the Coco Pops monkey that I gave to my dad, and he kept it in his diary for years.

I will come back to my art later, in particular how it helps me stay in tune with nature and the wildlife around me. When I am at the farm, I will often go down to the ancient woodlands or sit at the top of the valley looking across that spectacular view . . . and just sketch what I see. Sometimes it is a wide landscape, other times it might be a bird, a vole or even a leaf. Being around nature like that inspires me to draw and, in turn, sketching these amazing natural wonders allows me to study and learn about it from a totally different perspective.

Gymnastics also allowed me self-expression without any worries about words. It was immensely liberating. Perhaps understandably, I immediately poured all my energies into gymnastics and, looking back, really applied myself for such a young lad. I would watch the older, more experienced gymnasts doing a particular somersault or technique and I'd analyse how they did that, how they moved their body, how they landed, and then I would set about copying – and improving on – what I had seen. I seemed to have a good instinct for replicating and mimicking someone else.

I love the challenge of trying to do something that I have seen somebody else do – ever since I was a young lad, Dad's always said to me, 'Matthew, if somebody else is doing it, then there is no reason why you can't.' So, I love to look at someone doing something fantastic and be inspired by that, then go and try and do it for myself. I like to break each challenge down into milestones, then just spend my time mastering each individual stage, until I can do the entire task. Mind you, I always seem to end up doing it my own way, although whether or not I end up doing it better is another matter! Anyway, that is how I approached gymnastics – admittedly, at such a young age, I wasn't perhaps so conscious of what I was doing, but mimicking and trying to improve on the skills of others worked for me very well back then.

That's not to say I didn't have my fair share of tumbles – as a novice, you obviously have a lot of mishaps, that's all part of learning and improving, but there were obviously crash mats everywhere. I just threw myself into every new technique and went for it!

Mr Mullaney turned out to be massively influential in my career because although I only trained with him for a short while, he must've seen something in me. One evening he took my parents to one side and said, 'Matthew has got something, he needs to go elsewhere . . .' I will be forever grateful to him for that. It's funny, isn't it, how you get certain individuals in your life, sometimes for just a fleeting moment, who can have a really big impact. If it wasn't for him seeing something in me back then, my gymnastics would never have improved the way it did, and subsequently I would never have made it into television and the media, and done all the crazy stuff I've been lucky enough to do. I wouldn't even be writing this book . . .

Anyway, with Mr Mullaney's encouragement, I moved up to a leisure centre called Billingham Forum and my gymnastics career progressed very rapidly. As well as the obvious physicality, gymnastics also helped my young personality develop: I started socializing with people who were quite a bit older than me and that undoubtedly helped me with not being afraid to talk to anybody.

With the help of another wonderful coach called Peter Crawford, I progressed very quickly through the ranks of junior gymnastics. Something just clicked inside me: gymnastics felt really natural; every day I was desperate to go training. I didn't need pushy parents, I was always waiting to get in the car and go. I even set up this bar across my bedroom door to practise even more – although one day my mum came in with a basket of washing, smacked her head on it and actually knocked herself out! Probably with that in mind, one day my dad came back from a local auction – he loves his auctions and buys all sorts of bits and bats! – and said, 'Matthew, you'll never guess what I've bought!' Turned out he'd bought an entire high school gym! Parallel bars, a vaulting box, a high bar, all sorts of useful stuff. He'd only gone to the auction to buy some crash mats but he ended up bidding on everything! That was just the best day, to actually have that set up in one of our outbuildings was amazing and, of course, it made training so much easier.

The next move was to train at the Centre of Excellence in Middlesbrough, which was a big step-up because some of the older lads there were in the British squad, so there was a lot of hero-worship going on from me. Some of them really were the most incredible gymnasts. At such a young age it was so good for me to be around these very talented lads. I learned so much just from watching them, talking to them, getting tips or even pats on my back from them. They were driven, focused, determined – such brilliant role models for me at that age. In my eyes, they could do the seemingly impossible; it was like training alongside superheroes and I worked incredibly hard to do what I could to reach their level. I was also constantly entering competitions and I enjoyed some pretty decent success. I was North of England Champion for seven years and it wasn't long before I was winning medals at national championships and spending my summers training with the national squad.

I was only twelve, but I was always pushing to get better and better every day. One of my greatest achievements while I was doing gymnastics was being awarded a perfect ten at Lilleshall, which is the National Sports Centre and the HQ of British Gymnastics. The perfect score came on the floor, for what is known as a 'conditioning set', which is a collection of moves to show your gymnastic ability, range of movement, strength and pretty much everything that gymnastics encompasses. So to get a perfect ten in that was really quite something.

On the day of the performance, I felt really good as I started; even my salute, where you raise your arm up at the beginning of the routine, was sharp and focused. I was so determined and 'present' that I can almost put myself back there right now. I can feel my toes pointing so much to get the perfect form that tension ran all the way down the muscles in my legs. I held every single move for just that tiny split second longer than I needed to, because I knew that with nerves and excitement you often rush through your routine a little bit. I even got up from my final move slowly and very deliberately, no rush, composed and concentrating, because I wanted to savour every single element of the routine . . . then finished with a crisp, final salute at the end.

I sat down on the bench, put my tracksuit over my legs and just waited with my coach, Peter Crawford, for the judge's score. The judge was a man called Trevor Lowe and I can still see him there in his blue blazer and grey trousers as he walked back without much of an expression on his face at all . . . then he showed me the score . . . A PERFECT TEN!

I couldn't actually believe it. That was an incredible moment and one I am really, really proud of. Of all the things that I have achieved in my life, that one is really special. My coach Peter always used to say that everybody starts with ten and then marks are deducted from there. So the fact that the judge felt he couldn't take anything off as I went all the way through my routine was really something. Funnily enough, the perfectionist in me also remembers the next routine: everything was going incredibly well until right at the end when I pushed to go so high on a jump that I circled my arms around once more than I should have. The judge took 0.2 off and gave me a 9.8 for that routine. Still to this day, even as I recite this story, it pains me to remember that mistake because if I hadn't made that error, I'd be telling you that I got two perfect tens, one after the other!

That said, as a perfectionist, I always like to push and push and push, but, of course, in life it is very difficult to achieve perfection in any project or goal. So to be given a 'perfect ten' was something I was extremely proud of. Still am.

Now, for as long as I could remember, Mum had craved moving to a bigger farm. She was *desperate* to live out her dream and throw herself into the farming lifestyle completely. Mum went off to agricultural college to educate herself about all the complexities of running a farm and my parents spent every waking hour planning an upgrade to a fully fledged set-up. They heard about an old, disused farm that was coming up for sale west of Durham. It dated back to the 1600s and had some history as a dairy farm, but at the time they saw it, the place was actually owned by the Coal Board, and had been used as part of their work in the mines around the north-east. However, it had been disused for many years and, by the time my parents came across it, the place was boarded up, in fact pretty much all the windows were bricked up. Many of the outbuildings were falling down. This farm was in a really sorry state of disrepair.

Coal had been a very rich resource in and around County Durham and was mined in the area for centuries, as far back as medieval times. During the

Industrial Revolution, many of the county's most affluent people made their fortune from collieries and mining. From the 1850s, some of the mining locally had been done by a family of Darlington Quakers. In fact, that family was responsible for many of the mining villages in the area, including the one nearest to where our farm is located, which sprang up to provide housing for the workforce of these big mines. By 1923, there were said to be over 170,000 miners working in the county. Most were based at deep mines extracting coal from seams way below the surface, but around some areas, such as our farm, there were minerals much closer to the surface, so these were exploited using 'open-cast' methods. In more modern times, the industry has petered out locally, with the 1950s and 1960s seeing most pits closing; the last colliery in the Durham coalfield closed in 1994.

My mum and dad went to view the ramshackle farm, which sat overlooking a beautiful valley set in a hundred acres of fields, as well as an ancient woodland.

When they got there, it was in an even worse state than they had imagined.

They bought it *without even going inside*.

My family then upped sticks and moved into this remote farm, even though large parts of it were essentially uninhabitable. As a young lad, I had loved living on the smallholding, but this farm was something much, *much* bigger . . . and much more exciting. My parents had set off on this crazy journey, and me and my sister were along for the ride!

And do you know what?

I couldn't have been happier.

I was young when my parents moved into the farm, but I still have some really strong memories of those early days in the valley. One of my earliest recollections is when the house was still a shell with the windows all bricked up. Mum had been off to market and bought some sheep to start a flock, and we were heading into lambing season. We had no central heating and no cooker, and I vividly remember sitting by the fire eating Harvest Crunch cereal out of plastic camping bowls, which was just an easy way to get some energy without having a cooker. We did that first season of lambing fuelled on Harvest Crunch and sleeping on lilos!

As the evening wore on, it obviously got darker and darker, but because we hadn't yet been hooked up to the electricity properly, eventually we were pretty much sitting there in the pitch black. We settled down on our lilos and fell fast asleep, then woke with a start when the telephone rang in the other room. We were desperately trying to find the door, scrambling and stumbling around in the dark. Eventually, I found the door frame and flicked the light switch for a tiny bulb that somehow worked and when I switched it on, my mum was standing there, patting the chimney breast on the opposite side of the room, literally about to walk into the fireplace!

My parents started off by getting the farmhouse reconnected to all the essential utilities, which had been cut off years before. Obviously, the remote location meant this was not an easy task, but they persevered and eventually got sorted with drainage, water and power. Nothing is on the mains, it is all septic tanks and bottled gas, naturally.

There was a real sense of hunkering down as a family, rebuilding this beautiful old farmhouse and making it our own – feathering our nest. Over the years, that has brought us all a very real and proud sense of achievement. I actually learned a lot of my practical building skills through renovating the farm. Dad was brilliant. Like I said, he was a newsagent by trade but in his younger days was also a very skilled self-taught builder; he just used to figure out how to do a job and then do it. That ethos has stuck with me – we always say, 'Have a go yourself, and if it goes wrong, then get a builder in . . . but have a go yourself first.' That really is a farming mentality, that approach: figure something out yourself and fix it. It's born out of not being cost- or time-effective to always just hire people in, but there's also a rewarding sense of achievement in doing these tasks yourself.

Over the coming years, I gradually became confident at all sorts of building, roofing, brickwork, tiling, carpentry, remortaring. Outdoors there are loads of jobs that I will have a go at; obviously you become pretty adept at fencing when you live on a farm, fixing gates and water troughs, laying new piping for water supplies, repairing sheep pens, tinkering with machinery, all of that. I've always loved pouring myself into learning new skills and the farm was a perfect place to start! Of course, with some jobs you do have to recognize that you need an expert. The only things I don't really do are electrics and plumbing, but everything else is fair game.

With the farm being so remote, we live this quite solitary lifestyle, so we don't mind if our gutters are a bit wonky or if a roof tile is a bit lopsided – no one is really up there to notice anyway! Living where we do, it is much more about practicality; if the roof doesn't look like it's from an oil painting but also won't leak, then that works.

For all the hard work, I absolutely loved living on the farm. I had this whole new world at my fingertips, a world of discovery and learning that came at an age when I was so receptive and also able to help. What better playground for an inquisitive, practical lad than a hundred-acre farm!

With that wonderful childhood privilege in mind, let's start the tour of our farm through the seasons, beginning with the most energizing, exciting and vibrant few months you could wish for – spring!

2

# Spring

Spring is just the most beautiful, invigorating time on our farm. I love the sense that the farm and all its wildlife are waking up from the winter months. Everything is bursting into life and so springtime on the farm always generates this incredible feeling of being *engulfed* in all of nature's beauty. You are seeing the budding of the trees and the unfurling of their leaves as they open up, the flowers and plants shooting skywards, the winter browns turning to vivid greens; your whole environment suddenly becomes so stunningly vibrant. Spring is something that I long for, because the winters on the farm are intense: they're muddy, dark, cold, windy – not for the faint-hearted! When spring begins to arrive, that freshness and buoyancy I feel is tangible. I literally bounce as I walk around the farm – it is an exciting and life-affirming time of year.

You know when you hear a song that envelops you and is so emotive that it makes you feel really happy? That's what spring feels like for me, with everything coming out of hibernation. As the farm is so remote, this intense experience is even more special, because we are the only people here to witness what's going on. After the challenges of winter, when sometimes you are being battered by wind or hail, you're cold, muddy and exhausted and occasionally question why you are doing what you are doing, you never doubt yourself once spring returns . . . Spring always reminds me *why* we live somewhere like this farm and makes me feel ALIVE and so very thankful.

I love waking up really early in springtime and getting out at first light. It's magical. The crisp spring mornings are so energizing: I can look out across the valley and it just fills me with a love of life, every time. You don't have to scour around for signs of spring, either. You scan the view and start to see the landscape beginning to change colour. Nowhere is this more apparent than in our wonderful ancient woodland.

The woodland is down at the bottom of the valley slope, and if you stand on the doorstep of the farmhouse, you can see the treetops, which act as a great barometer of how spring is progressing. You can watch the ancient woodland as it turns from the brown, dark tones of winter, almost asleep, totally dormant . . . and then suddenly you notice this green haze appear and it's as if a signal has been given that the natural world is on its way back!

We are incredibly proud and protective of our woodland and I love spending time there. It really is a pleasure, and if I was to take you for a walk down there as spring arrives, you'd enjoy an intense experience that appeals to all of your senses. The springtime bluebells are just this breathtaking carpet of colour, it almost stops your heart when you wander in there and see all of that vibrant colour just covering the woodland floor. You will also come across wood anemones, speedwell, honeysuckle, primrose and wild garlic, the latter of which has the most beautiful aroma as you go down in there and catch the smell on the breeze. When the shards of sunlight pierce through the branches and light up all these plants and the woods themselves, it's absolutely magical.

Our ancient woodland is just this fascinating ecosystem, a whole other world that I love to be immersed in. In fact, ancient woodlands are home to more threatened species than any other environment. The centuries of life sustained in these wonderful woods create the most incredible diversity of species, whether that's huge communities of fungi, plants, insects, animals, birds or micro-organisms. Some of these species are regarded as 'indicators' that offer clues as to the age of the woodland. For example, lichen can offer a really good gauge of a woodland's age – we have loads of that – but other species can help with dating the area too, even slugs!

The fungi always take me back to my childhood. During summer holidays I would spend one morning a week down the local woodland at a wildlife group based there and we used to learn loads about the trees and different habitats that were around. We would forage for wild food and eat peppery wood sorrel. I also developed a fascination with fungi.

Today, I absolutely love to see the different species of fungi that crop up on the woodland floor or the bracket fungi that attach to trees. One of my earliest memories of moving to the farm was having a world of discovery and exploration to myself, where I could climb any of these trees that I wanted to and build dens to my heart's content.

When I was a young lad, I used to sit in a big old oak tree; I had a rope ladder that went to a big fork in the branches and acted as a base to look out or climb from. I would sit there for hours just looking down on the world below and putting everything into perspective. I used to climb as high as I could and I always remember feeling extreme excitement and trepidation as I got higher and higher, contemplating the challenges that I was going to face trying to get down again. Looking back now, those were hours well spent, sorting out my stuff with a life skill thrown in for good measure . . . I miss that rope ladder.

In our woods, we have self-seeded silver birch, alder, rowan, mountain ash, holly and some very old oaks, a few of which we believe to be hundreds of years old (some of the oldest in Durham, actually). We also have sessile oaks, which are slightly different to normal oak – they have stalkless acorns (that is the sessile part). It has a more upright trunk and straighter branches than an English oak and the leaves have longer stalks; interestingly, the two species often hybridize. I love an oak tree; there is something incredible about a gnarly old oak with huge limbs – they are so imposing and grandiose. According to the Woodland Trust, a single oak can produce as many as five million acorns!

As mighty as the oaks are, you do have to keep an eye on their structure once they are so old: some limbs need propping up; others put the tree at risk of toppling over in a storm. If you see a limb that is literally about to split the tree in half and therefore shorten the life of that oak, then you have to take action. I don't think you can be careful enough with these old oaks ; they are veterans of the countryside, they are a life-support system for so many species (some sources suggest up to 2300 species per oak) and so they deserve our care and attention.

One really old oak in our woodland was hit by lightning a few years back. (We do get quite a few lightning strikes – Mum and Dad hid under the kitchen table once after the farmhouse was hit!) The problem with the woodland is that it's located at the bottom of a steep valley side – so not only does that mean it can suffer from some pretty savage winds, but also when there is damage caused by a storm, extracting a fallen tree is a very tricky challenge because there is simply no access for modern machinery. Therefore, we often call upon more traditional methods to help.

The oak tree that was struck by lightning was completely felled and needed to be dealt with. This tree was massive, and there was no way you could move it without help. So, we brought in a horse logger called Chris with his North Swedish draught horse, Ole – a beauty, this absolutely massive, rusty brown giant of a horse.

We'd previously cut the tree up into manageable pieces and the horse was fitted with his special harness. Ole had two modes, resting quietly and working explosively! He just stood as calm and as peaceful as you like, gentle, hardly moving, standing there serenely. However, once Chris had finished attaching the chains to the log and given the command to start pulling, my word, suddenly he burst into gear, and that's when we got to see the immense, awe-inspiring power of a working draught horse. These were *big* logs, you wouldn't even be able to roll them yourself, and yet he was powering up the hill, in his element, dragging these massive sections of oak behind him. It was spectacular to watch. His breath was snorting out of his nostrils in the crisp air, you could see his huge muscular frame tensing and straining; the power was just incredible. (Remarkably, despite their size, North Swedish draught horses are relatively small for the species!)

It took Ole and Chris about half a day to get all of this enormous old tree dragged up and out of the woods. The point of using such traditional methods is twofold: as I mentioned, using mechanized machines isn't an option, due to the location of the woods, but also this more old-fashioned approach protects the habitat. The horse does the job without destroying any of the woodland floor, which is such a delicate environment – there are so many rich habitats down there that a digger would just decimate. Ole just made his way in and out of the trees with each log without really making a mark. The only evidence that he had been there were a few scrapes on the grass where the logs were pulled out, which obviously soon recovered and grew back.

Working in such a very old-school manner down in the woods was a lovely experience. I felt at one with the woodland, even to the point that lots of birds and wildlife came up to see what was going on; they were almost drawn to the energy of this horse. Also, the fact that we were working so closely alongside this beautiful, powerful animal was very special. I have a very close connection with horses, which I will come back to later, but wider than that, working with and around animals gives you that sense of being at one with them and nature, a theme we will also keep returning to.

These working horses are amazing. They understand how they can help, and in return you sense what they want to do for you: that is something I really enjoy . . . and they seem to really love it! I can tell you that if a horse as colossal as Ole didn't want to do something, you wouldn't be able to make him! You are both just working together, enjoying the process and being a team. It's wonderful.

As well as jobs such as this logging challenge, the woodland actually needs a lot of delicate management that really makes a difference and allows the plant life to thrive. One crucial element is the amount of light down there – we have opened up large sections to let in more light; this in turn allows more species to thrive, otherwise you are in danger of the woodland almost throttling itself. You might think, *That is a wild wood, wouldn't it be better if you just left it alone?* but the short answer is 'no'. That would just lead to the equivalent of a badly overgrown garden. Nothing would blossom because there wouldn't be enough light. So we remove encroaching vegetation and non-native, self-seeding trees and create new glades which are basically openings in a woodland that let the light in and allow the woodland floor to flourish. The colours you come across in a glade are stunning; a personal favourite is the vivid green of the grass – it is so striking and lush. Being at the bottom of the valley means our woodland can be quite damp for parts of the year, so there is no chance of the grass drying out. And the consequence, if you provide the grass with a plentiful supply of water and lots of sunshine . . . well, the results are *spectacular*.

Once you have managed the area to get all that beautiful light in, the grass can really prosper, and therefore in the depths of winter we let the sheep wander in and help themselves to some nutritious grazing. This also offers them shelter under the trees, which is really useful; that said, you have to really keep a careful eye out on the sheep once they are in the woods – it is quite a distance from the farmhouse, down at the bottom of the slope, and it is all too easy for them to get trapped in the undergrowth, such as on the dog roses for example. Once the thorns grab their fleece, they are stuck, and if we aren't aware then they can deteriorate and die in a very short space of time.

Set against the vivid green grass is a beautiful backdrop of silver birch, with their lovely lime-coloured leaves, shining in the dappled light. There will be pockets of white or black sheep grazing underneath and, depending on what time of year it is, they will be nestling in snowdrops or bluebells, purples and blues splashed across their feet; it really is like an artist's colour palette. Just magical.

And let's not forget the headline spring flower – the daffodil. There's nothing more invigorating after a long, dark winter than to see thousands of daffodils signalling the onset of spring. It always amazes me, the differences between parts of the UK; I might have friends down south whose daffodils are dying off, yet up here ours are only just appearing. We are so lucky to have such magnificent native species just popping up all over our island! We have daffodils all the way up the track and they've always reminded me of landing lights on a runway signalling the path home.

As well as opening up new glades, we also dug a pond down in the woodlands, too. Technically, this is known as a 'scraping' (essentially it's a big old hole in the ground!) and it's an interesting concept. We don't have rivers or streams on the farm, so our woodland pond is fed by field drains from a drainage system that makes the most of the enormous amount of run-off we get, being a steep valley. We managed to get a small digger down into the woodland, scraped away the surface, then we simply let Mother Nature take its course. If you take a woodland like this and introduce water, suddenly a whole new amount of life can come to live with you. In terms of planting new species, that pond area has self-seeded – we didn't put in a single thing, it's all entirely natural. Then we added in some extra habitats alongside what had taken root, and created a little beach area so that when the water level rises, it laps on the beach and creates a perfect haven for toads, dragonflies, water nymphs, larvae, mayflies and all sorts of other insects . . . the whole place is alive!

In some senses, the woodland requires more management than the farm itself. The problem for many people with ancient woodlands is that the costs of that management can be very extensive while the return can be very little, or nothing at all. Not everyone is in a position to preserve and manage these beautiful woodlands, so it is a real dilemma.

If you are managing an ancient woodland to make money, that is never going to work out. If you want to turn woods into cash, you need to be in a different game altogether. Recently, we have seen a lot of new woodland sprouting up due to the offset of carbon emissions. When you see these really dense forests of conifers, those very high trees that are planted incredibly tightly, they are essentially being farmed the same way that you might do with barley. Although, of course, barley is harvested every year, whereas forestry wood can take thirty years plus to grow!

In our small woods, we are able to harvest some firewood and use the wood in certain ways – that was the traditional purpose of many woodlands. We also coppice where appropriate, which is the art of chopping one branch to create two. My dad taught me how to turn wood as well, so we are able to make things with timber from our own woodland. And, of course, we are absolutely dedicated to helping the thousands of species that live there to continue to do so.

The Woodland Trust define 'ancient' as 'areas of woodland that have persisted since 1600 in England and Wales, and 1750 in Scotland'. Due to their age, precious rarity and biodiversity, these ancient woodlands are extremely valuable to our countryside and desperately need to be protected. You can't just plant a 'new' woodland like ours, the richness and biodiversity in there has evolved over centuries. According to sources, just 2.5 per cent of UK land is covered by ancient woodlands, less than 610,000 hectares. That's really worrying, because once they are gone, they're 'gone for good'. I am delighted to say that in the UK we have actually mapped all the known sites in the country, which are recorded in a central inventory, giving details of the species, layout and other useful information. For example, Sherwood Forest is the largest concentration of ancient oaks in northern Europe, boasting nearly one thousand trees, some of which are up to a millennium old. There are different categories of ancient woodland – a common type would be what are known as 'semi-natural woods', which have developed naturally but have been used by us humans, perhaps for timber, for example, over many centuries, and have had substantial woodland cover for more than four hundred years.

One notion that I love to think about is the tradition that when knights of old passed away, sometimes the elders would ride out to the fringes of the city, such as nearby Durham, and plant an oak sapling in honour of the fallen hero. Who knows who might have been remembered in this way down in our woodland?

Of course, it's not just the plant life that re-emerges from the dark winter months into a burst of spring and new life, nor is it only something that you see down in the woodlands. The animals that we live with on the farm also start to reappear in every corner and everywhere you look. Suddenly, you see hares bounding across the ground, you see deer jumping over fences, you get those heart-warming moments when you hear the curlew cry as it comes back to the farm, and you marvel as the returning swallows swoop overhead on their way back from their overseas wintering grounds. In springtime, everything is back, everything's ready to party and our farm is the place to be!

I love that springtime is so busy with all the individual species – I can walk around the farm and woodland and feel this real, natural sense of community within the landscape. It's not about the people, it's about this energy, this sense of the natural world. Without wanting to get too romantic about it, in spring I literally walk around the farm and feel like I am one of *them*; I get an intense joy from this season. To experience this wave of energy coming from the trees and the foliage and the animals and the insects and the weather . . . just all of it! I relish having their company after not having seen so many of them for months. If you just sit down and stay quiet and steady long enough, all sorts of animals will start to come out to see you.

One lovely resident of the ancient woodlands that we are waiting to be confirmed as living here is the dormouse. That species is really very rare around where we live. A few years ago, down by the pond in the woods, we noticed some nuts that had been eaten in a certain way which is very characteristic of the dormouse and how they nibble their food. They hold them in their grip and then nibble round in a very specific circular motion. We sent these half-eaten nuts off to be analysed but those tests were inconclusive. Undeterred, we put some boxes out in the woods, a little bit like bird boxes but with certain sections inside that dormice will love, to create a perfect nesting habitat for that tiny species. Then we waited and waited and waited; we've had no luck yet – mind you, we did find a nest that turned out to be a wood mouse. So we are still wondering if dormice have moved in with us . . . and that is all part of the magic of trying to provide somewhere for creatures to live. You never know what is going to happen! I love that feeling of creating an environment, an opportunity for certain creatures to live a lovely life, then sitting back and waiting to see if they decide to move in.

There is one literal display of new life which happens every spring that is my favourite part of that season, and just a joy to be around: lambing. Each year, farmers have to care for over fifteen million ewes giving birth. Although lambing starts as early as December in some areas, as a general rule it is during the spring, around February to April. I will explain about the art of 'tupping' – putting your male sheep (a 'tup') in with the ewes to breed – later in the autumn section of this book, but for the purposes of this spring chapter, you need to know that if you put your tups in with the ewes on Bonfire Night, you will definitely get plenty of fireworks! The gestation period means that you will then get your lambs on 1 April, or, as the old saying goes, 'In with a bang and out like fools!'

Along the course of the ewe's pregnancy, the modern farmer will have a lot of technology at their disposal, like scanning. Typically, the ewes are scanned around forty to ninety days after tupping, mainly to see if they are pregnant, but also to see how many lambs are on board, so we can provide them with the best possible nutrition going forward. Also, you can alter the feed very accurately if there is a ewe who is showing signs of certain deficiencies or is perhaps carrying triplets and therefore needs more nourishment, and so on.

When the end of the gestation period is approaching, you really have to ramp up your vigilance of the ewes. You make sure that each one has all the care and attention that she needs. We often put all the ewes who are carrying singles, twins or triplets in different areas to help us manage them more precisely. (Triplets are pretty rare, and quadruplets even more unusual!)

Once the time comes for the ewe to give birth, we will always try to let the natural way take its course. Depending on the breed, some ewes will deliver their lambs on their own in a field somewhere out of the way; we house our Hampshire Down sheep in a poly-tunnel so we can keep a closer eye on them. It's a brilliant ventilated environment with open ends. Up here, it is not uncommon to have snow at Easter, a late burst of winter, and even not unheard-of to be completely snowed in at that time. For that reason, you might choose to lamb inside. It isn't just the extremes of snow that might make shelter necessary – indoor lambing will also protect the young from the prevailing winds, because if the wind hits lambs when they are already wet, they can get cold really quickly and you can lose them in what feels like moments.

Indoor lambing pens create work, because you need to constantly provide water and feed. Our hardier breeds – the Hebrideans, the Herdwicks, the Cheviots and the Black Welsh Mountain sheep – are much more self-sufficient in that sense because you can leave them outside during lambing, which is much less hands-on. Either way, we like to keep a very close watch over all the ewes during this time, in case anything goes wrong. That can be very tiring, because the ewes obviously don't lamb only in working hours or when it is convenient to you; sometimes you might get a new arrival in the early hours of the morning and at the bottom of a very dark field!

The first signs you will get that the ewe is about to give birth will be when she starts pacing and pawing the ground. You'll then see what looks almost like a clear bag – known as the 'water bag'. This bag comes first and that's the moment that you know the arrival is imminent. The ewe will start to lick her mouth, lift her head up and start to push . . . the contractions are making her do this. Soon after, she will be really arching her back to help push the lamb out.

What you are hoping, and looking for, is a lamb in a diving position – so ideally two toes and a nose coming out of the back end of the ewe first, its front feet pointing forward and its head resting on its forelegs. One part of this amazing birthing process is looking for what we call 'the golden hoof', because there are little yellow tips on the front of their hoofs as they come out. If the lamb is in the diving position, all good, you can let the ewe push it out and the whole event usually happens very smoothly.

However, if there is just one leg out front or maybe only a leg and no head showing, then that means the neck is potentially stuck behind the birth canal – that is the point when you need to intervene. A breech can be fatal for both the mum and the lamb, so you need to act fast if you think something is wrong. There's no pleasant way to say this, but you put your hand in there and feel around, trying to establish the lamb's position so you can readjust it inside the mum and help it come out safely . . . *Ah, there's the other foot and . . . now I've got the nose . . .* with the aim being to put the legs and nose back into the birth canal in the correct alignment and, in so doing, help the lamb slide out. You are aiming for a smooth passage through the birth canal and if that has to involve you putting your own hand in there, then so be it.

Once the lamb is safely out, you leave them to bond. Lambs typically weigh around 4–5 kg at birth, but obviously that depends on the breed. As soon as they are born, it is amazing how Mother Nature takes over and the mums are instantly into cleaning, cleaning, cleaning. They clean around the nose first of all, to help their new arrival breathe. Occasionally, you sometimes need to give a little pat on the tummy to get a lamb's heart going and to jump-start the breathing. Every now and then you have to clear the air passage with a little piece of straw up their nose and help clear the mouth – that's usually all it takes. You hear a little cough, they will shake themselves, flap their ears about and then you know that all is good. If you have used scans (which we tend to do less nowadays than we have in the past), you should know if another lamb is on the way out or not. But you can normally tell by the ewe's size, age and previous lambing history if she's about to have another.

From the time the lamb is born to it being up on its feet and having a drink from its mum is incredibly quick. The ewe's teats have a natural wax-like seal that you can help to break to get the milk flowing so that the newborn lamb can drink. Usually the lamb will dislodge this when it first drinks, but you can remove it by hand. You need to make sure that the lamb is drinking well and getting the colostrum, which is a nutrient-rich initial milk that the ewe will produce at this very early stage. Colostrum is full of antibodies – while the lamb was inside its mother, it was protected by her antibodies, but now it is out in the big wide world, it needs its own immunity, so colostrum really is a superfood. For those indoors that we can grab, we also dip the navel in iodine to prevent infection.

The wonders of Mother Nature mean that once we are happy with our polytunnel lambs, we can turn the newborns out into the field with their mother within as little as twelve hours of being born (if the weather is onside, of course). For the breeds lambing outside, it's wonderful to observe the whole process from a distance . . . incredible!

Whilst watching ewes and lambs out in the fields, you will often see a ewe turn around and sniff a lamb's back end as it arrives for a drink – this is because it can smell its own milk passing through the lamb, and that way they are reassured that it's their offspring. Over the coming months, again depending on the breed and the environment, the lambs gradually come off the milk and end up on a grass diet.

There is a fascinating process called fostering as well, where maybe you have ended up with an extra lamb for whatever reason – maybe Mum isn't around, maybe she has died or maybe there are triplets that the mum can't look after all at the same time. When this happens, you take one lamb and you give it to a mother with a single, so she ends up with twins. You can foster them on, so if you can get the milk of the new ewe through the unrelated lamb, you can actually make the ewe think that it's her newborn. There are various different ways of doing that, such as having the ewe feeding in a special crate while the new lamb suckles, and after a couple of days or so, the ewe smells her own milk and fosters the lamb as her own. Slightly more messy is the option to smear the lamb with afterbirth, which the ewe will then lick off so the bonding can happen that way.

A hardier breed such as the Herdwicks are much more self-sufficient with their lambing. They can lamb outside no problem. Even so, we move them to a front field that is visible from the house, so it is easy to keep a close eye on them when lambing time arrives. We have also put a field shelter to the left-hand side so that if the weather turns, they can go and find their own protection from the elements. The first time we provided that 'accommodation', quite a few of the Herdwicks actually wandered into the field shelter under their own devices to lamb in there, which was magical to watch. Mostly, they seem to go in there for shelter from the direct sunshine and heat; if it's snowing and windy or raining, they tend to stay outside! Similarly, the black Hebrideans that we've had for a long time will often lamb themselves down in the woods; they disappear off down there and come back a little while later with two tiny lambs in tow! They much prefer to be on their own. Their lambs are really tiny, but so capable; they are my wife Nicola's favourite lambs (I'm a big fan, too) and she absolutely loves to see those little lambs!

Of course, as much as lambing is mostly a joyous time, it can sadly come with complications. Every time you welcome new life, there are going to be risks, such as when you lose a newborn. This is never nice to witness, but even then, you have to keep the loss in context. Farm life is not just about learning how to put up a fence, shear sheep or feed livestock. It teaches you so much about life in general. For example, one aspect that you learn very young on a farm is that 'where there's livestock, there's deadstock'. I'll tell you something: that is one of the biggest lessons you will learn on a farm. It is all lovely and exciting and rewarding when things are going well, but there is a side to farming – and life – that is less idyllic. I remember during lambing season after we'd just lost a lamb at birth, I asked my mum, 'Can't we do anything to save it?' I really believed it would be possible to bring it back to life but it was too late, she had tried and it just hadn't worked. Fast forward three decades and my daughter Molly said exactly the same words to me after we lost a lamb, too. Literally the same question in the same scenario. We had tried all sorts to bring this little lamb back to life but to no avail. As an experienced adult, there is a moment when you look and realize that you can't do any more. We talked about what had happened that day and I could just tell that Molly 'got it'. Harsh as that sounds, she had learned the lesson. Molly was really sad and upset, but you can't shield your children from it. It's not ideal and it's not nice, but it is real life.

In my opinion, you can learn everything in life from being on a farm. No doubt about it. I honestly believe that. It prepares you for everything. I love that my children can help with lambing and I know they will learn so much about life outside of the farm by doing so.

Although lambing sounds pretty full on and hectic – and it is! – I love the calmness at the end of a day of lambing. I love making sure that the animals are all OK and everything is cared for and sorted and fed and watered and happy and safe. Plus, I never tire of seeing the birth of a lamb and watching new life coming into this world. I also adore watching natural instinct at work – it is just incredible when you see a little lamb wobble to its feet only a few minutes after being born, looking for a drink and fending for itself, surviving. You know you still have a lot of work to do, you will be checking in on them through the night, so the job is not done, but it is a remarkably rewarding feeling to get to the end of a successful day lambing. Then, the next morning, there is a real energy as you get up, an intense feeling of excitement about the new arrivals that never fails to invigorate me. You turn them out into the fields and get to see them experiencing things for the first time: the grass, socializing with one another – they all run up and down the hedge line together; it is like a lamb Grand National, purely on instinct.

Lambing is just the most wonderful period on the

farm. You are quite literally seeing new life arrive and no matter how many times I am involved with the process, I find it a joyous experience. Year after year, time after time, despite all the hard work, late nights and occasional slippery, sticky forearm, lambing never ceases to take my breath away.

When I was in my teens, I used to love going round the farm in springtime on our quad bike, wandering in the meadows or just being around the livestock, the bursting plants and the amazing energy that the season brings. Combined with life on the farm, my gymnastics ensured that I was always very physically fit as a young lad – my secondary school, Belmont, was very sporty and all my friends were athletic and highly successful at a number of sports. The main one was ice hockey, in fact a lot of them played for Durham Wasps academy system and even Great Britain – it was a very healthy environment to be immersed in. I have good memories of that school.

At this point, I was working on a dairy farm on a weekend and I also did a milk round, so I would be up at half four every morning to deliver the milk to the whole village (for a fiver a morning and double milk on a Saturday). Then I would come home, get ready for school, go into class, train in the gym at lunchtime, come home, go to the gym again, then finally fall into my bed, exhausted, for a few hours' sleep before it all started again!

Although the money from the milk round wasn't really a driver for me, I did begin to earn a decent amount, so I used that to buy calves and rear them myself on powdered milk, then sell them at market. I started a little livestock venture aged fourteen. I tell you, I made some good money with that, I really did. When I think back, I did work bloody hard!

That period made me realize what you can achieve in one day. My mother has always been one for saying, 'Never waste the day'; that is a phrase that I have heard ever since I was little: 'Matthew, don't waste the day!' And she is right.

My gymnastics was getting better and better and I felt like I wanted to be involved with this sport for the rest of my life. Unfortunately, around the age of fourteen, I started to find myself very tired most of the time – now, previously this was not something I'd ever felt, I always had bags of energy. I was training hard and working all these other physical jobs, yes, but that was nothing new, so it was obvious that something wasn't right. Eventually I underwent all these tests and the doctors found out that I was anaemic. It wasn't threatening my health, but it was affecting the way that I was growing. The doctors sat me down and advised that the situation was manageable, provided I drop down to training two or maybe three times a week.

The problem was, at the level I was competing in gymnastics, that would simply not have been good enough. There was no way I could carry on winning and progressing if I was only training a few times a week. So, although it was a tough call to make, I took the decision to retire from gymnastics.

I was obviously pretty gutted. However, even as a young lad, I always thought long and hard about big decisions and then once I'd made my mind up, I was happy to stick with my choice. I've never been one to make a decision on a whim, I imagine every outcome possible first, I am a big over-thinker, so when I make a decision, I don't look back, I just go for it.

Therefore, I do remember feeling quite at ease once I had finally made the decision. I felt I could move on. So, after the initial upset, it wasn't a sad end to my gymnastics career at all, actually.

After my anaemia ended my gymnastics career prematurely, I looked around for other sports to throw myself into. I became North of England pole-vault champion, I was a hurdler and I also did Sports Acrobatics, which is like formation or team gymnastics, in a group. My team of four lads even became British Champions in that sport.

Many years later, just before I turned thirty, gymnastics came back to me when I started commentating for the BBC on the Olympics and the World Championships. I knew all the coaches at these competitions and I also knew how the competitors felt; it was my world, so I found that a very enjoyable and natural place to be.

I chuckle sometimes when I see a young footballer signing to a big club for £100,000 a week or whatever. Nobody spent more time training as a young lad than me; I didn't know anybody at my age that would spend the hours committed to a cause as I did with gymnastics. In that sense, if financial gain had been my priority, I couldn't have picked a worse sport to commit to. If I'd have put that amount of effort and time into football, well, I might've been a very wealthy young man! But I didn't do gymnastics for money, that never crossed my mind – I did it because I LOVED the sport. My parents have always taught me to follow my passions and that's exactly what gymnastics was.

Gymnastics taught me the recipe for life. That sport showed me that if you work really hard, put the hours in and graft, you *will* get results. It's a simple formula: work hard – always – and ask yourself if you are giving absolutely everything. *Can I give more? Can I try harder?* Gymnastics also taught me that even if you work hard and give something your absolute best, sometimes things go wrong but . . . you still try, because the rewards could be far greater than if you don't have a go. That sport taught me how to confront fear. I'm not saying I am fearless – far from it – but what gymnastics teaches you is that there are times when you are frightened, and times when you have to put your trust in other people – for example, Mr Mullaney, Mr Crawford and my other coaches, Craig Burton and Sean Potter – and also you have to trust that they have instilled the right techniques in you and that you know how to execute what you have been training for.

It is a fine line between 'That is brilliant!' and 'This is going to hurt!'

Gymnastics helped me know as a young lad that I could try 'scary' things, that I had the confidence to give things a go. It also taught me to take risks – even if sometimes those risks don't pay off.

Life is full of risks, after all.

And when something goes wrong, when you fall or stumble, you get up, dust yourself down, go again.

A fresh and exciting new life might be about to start up.

After the dark winter months, there is always a brighter spring around the corner . . .

# 3

# Sheep

Living on a farm means there is always something unexpected happening. Mother Nature makes sure that you never know what is round the corner – you can plan, schedule, prepare every year and every season, learn from past mistakes and improve all the time, but there is still always that random element that catches you off guard. In the summer of 2020, while the world was locked down in the middle of a pandemic, our farm in the Durham Dales threw a really nasty accident in the path of my family, which came as a great shock.

It was a normal weekday for me whilst living on our smallholding that we have in the Chilterns on the outskirts of London.

Then the phone rang.

It was my dad.

'Matt, it's your mum . . .'

It was one of those heart-in-mouth moments that you never forget.

'She's been in an accident . . . she's in hospital . . .'

It transpired that Mum had been down in the sheep pens, getting everything sorted for the shearer to come. She had been separating the sheep into different areas of the pens. It's something she has done without incident loads of times over many decades – a very normal, everyday part of life on any farm.

Unfortunately, that wasn't the case on this particular day.

As one especially large sheep was going through an open gate, this ewe suddenly decided she wanted to rejoin her flock. She bolted and charged flat out towards the opening and, as Mum was standing in her path, she smashed into her, BANG! . . . took her feet from under her and snapped her leg below the knee in the process. My mum is a strong, experienced shepherdess, but these sheep are around eighty kilos, so I'll tell you something, if they are running at you full pelt, then you don't want to be in the way.

She had no chance.

Mum was completely immobilized and in so much pain that she actually passed out.

Thank God, she wasn't on her own. Dad isn't able to help with the sheep due to his own health challenges, so he was up in the farmhouse, none the wiser. Luckily, Mum was down there with a local lad called Eddie who helps her out on a Saturday. She'd actually been in two minds as to whether she should ask Eddie to help. I dread to think what might've happened had she been alone.

With Mum on the ground and in extreme pain, Eddie immediately rang his dad Arnie, an ex-marine who knew exactly what to do in a situation like that. He drove straight over and helped Mum up. He took her back to the farmhouse up the hill, told my dad, who was obviously worried sick, then somehow got Mum into a car and drove her to hospital.

That's when Dad rang me. At that time, I had literally just left *The One Show* and was busy working with my new production company down south, rushing around, hectic. As soon as I put the phone down, my wife Nicola, along with our son Luke and daughter Molly, basically upped sticks with me straight away, chucked all of our animals – the sheep, chickens, the dog and cat – in a cattle trailer and drove north straight up the motorway to my parents' farm.

The next few hours were all such a blur, to be honest.

As soon as we got to the farm in the north-east, we amassed as much information as we could on what had happened and, more importantly in the immediate term, what Mum's injuries were. She had shattered her kneecap and fractured the top of her tibia, a very serious combination of injuries. Although Mum is really fit and strong for her age and certainly didn't need a knee replacement before the accident, the severity of her injuries was such that the doctors advised that she did indeed need a new knee. She would be convalescing for many months.

After we had done the firefighting in terms of Mum's immediate emergency and well-being, and knew she was settled and safe in hospital, we all sat down back at the farm, completely exhausted, and tried to take it all in.

I knew straight away that life on the farm had to change. The way that my parents choose to farm can be very demanding on them. Our hundred acres are all a thousand feet above sea level. It is very much a grazing farm, nothing arable, purely because the quality of the land that we have, along with the terrain, means arable farming would be very difficult. The climate can be pretty inclement – it is more wet than dry across any given year, and in the winter it can get viciously cold and harsh. Being a fully certified organic farm, they also do not use pesticides, medicines or other modern technologies that would make their life more convenient. Animal husbandry and organic farming is a passion but it is most definitely not the easy option.

What we did first was move back into the farm as a family, so that we could help Dad and, when she was eventually discharged from hospital a week after the accident, Mum too. Like I said, I wasn't on *The One Show* any more and the kids were on their school holidays, so we could literally just move back in lock, stock and barrel.

Mum made very speedy progress as her convalescence was aided brilliantly by Nicola, who is a trained physiotherapist. We were very fortunate to have her expertise to hand and that undoubtedly speeded up Mum's recovery. Given this was during the Covid pandemic, I have no idea how we would've coped if Mum had needed to go into hospital every few days for physio; in fact, given the strains on the NHS, the hospital wasn't doing any face-to-face consultations at all. Luckily, Nicola was able to facilitate the correct treatment by liaising with the hospital over the phone, which was incredibly helpful and we were all immensely grateful for that.

Due to the national lockdown, everybody was going through the worst time as a nation, so in many respects the challenges we were being faced with were nothing in comparison to what a lot of families had gone through. Nonetheless, we were in a situation where something needed to change and luckily we were in a position to make that happen.

With Mum back home, we started to formulate a plan about how we needed to alter the farm to ensure that my parents could continue to do what they love – live and work on their own organic farm, surrounded by animals and nature – but in a safe and less physically demanding manner.

One big part of that challenge was . . . you can't tell my mother what to do!

Well, you can, but she is set in her ways and – in her defence – is *very* PASSIONATE about what she does. It's one of the elements of her personality that we love so much. When you have put your heart and soul into a farm for decades, it is totally understandable that you like to operate in a certain way. Even so, and especially after such a horrendous trauma, I wasn't sure how she might react to our suggestions about lightening her workload.

As it happens, she was brilliant! We had a big sit-down talk and chatted through the ways that we felt the farm needed to change.

I said to her, 'You want to keep farming, you love the concept of the animal-husbandry side of this life, you want to do all those things and you don't want to stop, so actually let's fast-forward five years from now and think where do you want to be then? And how can we change it around now to ensure that will happen?'

Both of my parents said they absolutely did not want to move from the farm, so it was a case of changing the farm to create a new future for them both. Dad said he had worried for a number of years that something like the accident might happen. He is twelve years older than my mum, and he knows what it is like to be at that later stage in life, so he was very receptive to change, too.

Looking back, it was only ever going to be the sheep that told my mum the old ways needed to change . . .

. . . and trust me, she got the message.

We all knew the way that things had always been done in the past was no longer the way that we could do them in the future. The key was to change the way the farm was set up so that Mum could continue to have the life that she adores – spending time with the animals and looking after them all – but in a way that didn't present her with increasingly unrealistic physical demands and, indeed, risks. So, for example, it was never a case of no more sheep; it was a case of *different sheep*. She would never give up her animals, but maybe we could look at smaller and less dependent breeds. We were never going to suggest suddenly buying loads of massive modern farm equipment, or using pesticides and medicines to make her life easier, or sell off parts of the land, or bring in loads of contractors and technology.

However, we had to find ways of lightening her load.

As a family, we needed to create change, so we all pulled together and said, 'Right, let's find a sustainable way to move forward and turn this horrible accident into a huge positive!'

We sat down together and went through every single element of the farm and decided which areas could stay the same, and which needed to change. Throughout the pages of this book, you will see the plan that we have put in place and, as we move forward together as a family into the future, I very much hope that those ideas come to fruition. At the heart of what we are trying to do is the fact that my mum and dad have been through a lot in their lives and they know what they want to do above everything else – to live and work on their beautiful farm. Mum said that the accident made her feel vulnerable for the first time ever at the farm, and we simply could not allow her to feel like that ever again.

They have been such wonderful parents who have given me a great upbringing on the farm and the most amazing unwavering support at every twist and turn of my life and career.

I've always tried to do the same for them but this felt like a whole new level.

Now, it felt like the wave of responsibility was with me and I was determined to make their days easier and more enjoyable, just like they have done for me my entire life.

It was clear we needed to make some big changes and one of the first was in terms of the sheep. Over the years, we've had many different breeds of sheep on this farm anyway; to a degree, that is a natural part of the evolution of any farm: you adapt and change and try different approaches, either by design or sometimes out of necessity. When Mum was injured, it was clear that we needed to bring in different breeds for two principal reasons: (1) they needed to be lower maintenance and (2) they needed to be smaller. Now, don't be under any illusion that my mum is some kind of wallflower, she is a very strong, very capable shepherdess, but let me tell you from personal experience, when an eighty-kilo sheep bolts and smashes into you, it isn't pretty.

Sheep were one of the very first livestock animals to be domesticated, with evidence of various managed breeds as far back as 6000 BC or possibly even earlier. They are not actually originally native to the UK, but can be traced way back to related species in Mesopotamia around 11000 to 9000 BC. Their increased use in the UK mirrors the changing landscape of our island – where once the British Isles were covered in forest, over thousands of years the land was extensively cleared for agriculture and grazing. In the lower areas, it tended to be pigs and cattle, while sheep remained on the moorlands and heaths of higher altitudes. By the Bronze Age, sheep were a very common sight around the UK and soon became the dominant species for farming.

Over the centuries, the popularity of wool has gradually lessened (I will explain more about this in Chapter 4, 'Summer'), and so the needs of sheep farmers changed too, such that by the eighteenth century, breeds that produced good meat were starting to become increasingly popular. It's also really interesting to see that farmers were selectively breeding sheep hundreds of years ago, to try to create flocks that were more suited to the commercial demands at the time. For example, highland breeds are necessarily hardy and thrive on the vegetation of those areas which is said to 'impart a good flavour to the meat'. This breeding has continued at a pace – in 1800 there were about twenty breeds native to the UK, whereas in the modern day there are around thirty. Overall, the UK has 5 per cent of the world's sheep population, and over 20 per cent of the sheep in Europe, amounting to over twenty million head.

Of course, all my stories about sheep have to be read in the context of our small flocks. At the largest scale, we would've had around three hundred sheep, maximum; as I write, we are in the process of reducing to find the most sustainable number going forward. The average British sheep farmer will have considerably more and some of the biggest flocks can be thousands of animals strong, on farms that cover countless square miles.

The sheep we breed have to be very carefully selected due to the location and frequently inclement weather here – the Dales are not always perfect for sunbathing, let's put it like that! So we decided to bring in sheep from higher ground, because when you bring them to somewhere like this, they think it's the Caribbean! They're used to nibbling on very stubbly grasses up some mountainside, then suddenly they arrive here and have this amazing banquet of grass, you can literally see them thinking, *This is the life!*

So, how exactly did we change our sheep breeds after Mum's accident? Well, we went out and bought smaller breeds that also needed less hands-on maintenance, animals that could graze and lamb more independently of Mum, and were easier for her to handle.

Therefore, we changed the focus of the farm towards the breeds that will cope better here. For over twenty years, we've bred Hampshire Down and Hebridean sheep, both well-known heritage breeds. These are basically old-school sheep breeds that are native to the UK and were bred in certain parts of our landscape, hence they have names that are usually taken from counties or regions. Heritage breeds are from a different generation of farming – these days, farming has become more intense, it has become quicker, it has become ultra-competitive. Large heritage flocks are often slow growing, so that doesn't necessarily appeal to a farmer who is under such commercial pressure.

Heritage breeds have an innate ability to eat what you want them to eat and leave what you'd like them to leave. Heritage breeds also tend to be pretty resistant to disease; they are very self-sufficient, good at reproducing independently of us humans, and for much of the time can be left to their own devices, because they are basically bred to suit the landscape that they are on, with as little input from us as possible.

The goal for Mum has not been to sell for meat, she wants to sell the ewes, which will in turn go off and breed on other farms, while the males will be used for tupping elsewhere. She's worked over many years to create what is known as a 'closed flock'. This is when all the ewes have been bred by you, on your farm, and you are not buying in stock all the time. At that point, you've got your bloodline going forward and the aim is to breed really good ewes and really good rams, as breeding stock to be sold. That quality and authenticity of stock carries a premium and is much sought after. These are the real pure bred flocks that people are always keen to buy. However, this is not a fast option – for the bloodline of the new sheep that we brought in after her accident to be well established is likely to take around ten years.

Like Mum, I am really passionate about heritage breeds because I love the concept of having that connection with the farming generations before us. With regards to Hampshire Downs, Mum settled on this striking breed mostly because they are really more teddy bear than sheep and they proved to be a perfect choice. They became established in the first half of the nineteenth century by selective breeding of various breeds that were native to that region. Hampshires are a fantastic-looking sheep, with these woolly cheeks and a fleece that comes right down over their foreheads and almost round their eyes. Normally, shearers don't really enjoy working on such woolly breeds, but to be fair, it was our own shearer who recommended the Hampshires to Mum, so he can't complain!

Despite having spent a huge amount of time and focus on the Hampshire Down breed, we felt that, practically, they are not the best going forward and so our major plan has been to switch from breeding the Hampshire flock over to easier-to-manage heritage breeds. The Hampshires do need some looking after when the weather up here hits hard. They are used to the lowlands of those rolling Hampshire Downs, with all its lush green grass and milder climate. They aren't our smallest flock, either, with a large ram being as heavy as 125 kilos. So, although they look beautiful, they do create a lot of work and so that's the reason why we've decided to change direction to the hardier hill breeds.

A great example of this new direction is the fantastic flock of Black Welsh Mountain sheep we now have with us on the farm. Although we'd researched, looked into and spoken to people about this breed before we went to buy some, we hadn't really had a huge amount to do with them in the past. The main practical attraction for my mum was the fact that it's a small breed: they are quite compact, which obviously makes them easier for her to handle.

Myself, Nicola, Luke and Molly went to see them in Snowdonia (unfortunately Mum couldn't join us because of her leg), where they were grazing. The farmer with the flock we were seeing is a lady called Glenda and she brought them down off the mountain for us to have a look, right by this lake at the foot of Snowdon – what a setting!

She brought their mothers down for us to see while the tup was in the next paddock. This breed has a wonderful nature; I was really taken by their demeanour. Glenda put them in a pen, so we were walking around in there and they were all so calm, another good characteristic for my mum and her future management of the flock. Both my children and my mum are really keen on actually showing them, and it is a breed that my mum could quite easily take an example of into a ring or whatever and not have too much of a stressful, physical time with it if it decided that it wanted to go elsewhere. In fact, Nicola said that Black Mountain sheep are almost like the Labradors of the sheep world: they want to be with you, they are inquisitive yet quite methodical in the way that they interact with you – they are not going to suddenly run through you, let's put it like that, which is a welcome thought.

Gosh, the first thing that strikes you when you get up close to this breed is their eyes. They have a very crisp and clear eye in the way that they look at you; also they have these incredibly black faces and an intensely black fleece that is very deep inside. By 'deep inside', I mean once you look inside the fleece – just as with the Hebrideans – it's incredibly dark. The sun can tint these Black Mountain sheep's fleece a little, so they go a little bit browner in the sunshine, but when you get deep down in the fleece, it's really dark.

We bought shearlings from Glenda, which are a year old, so too young to put into lamb, but we were bringing them on to our farm at that age so that they could grow on and be with us for a while before we put them in lamb.

As well as their compact size and gentle nature, another big factor in buying some Black Mountain sheep was the fact they are a hardy breed that can cope well in a harsh climate. The high ground of Snowdonia can obviously be a pretty challenging environment at times and these Welsh Mountains were bred specifically for that landscape, so they are going to be very well suited to our farm.

Black Welsh Mountain sheep have a natural resist-
ance to some diseases, which helps us as an organic
farm because we aren't allowed to use a large number of modern medicines. They are easy-going, very
self-reliant and will happily munch on stubby grass
all day. Like many of our breeds, they make good
mothers and the lambs are quite strong and hardy
from birth. Their fleeces produce an appealing cloth
that is durable, light and warm.

I am actually really excited about what we potentially could do with the wool. Glenda was telling me
that there is a gentleman over in Germany who is
sourcing it for clothes and he is buying up all that he
can get his hands on, because it is such good quality.

One final note about these Black Mountain sheep
– I often talk about the fact that one of farming's
most rewarding elements is the idea that you are
part of generations of people working the land and
with animals. These methods, ideas and wisdoms get
passed down from generation to generation and to
be a small link in that lineage is an incredible privilege. With these Welsh sheep, we noticed straight
away that when Glenda called them over by rattling
a feed bucket, she spoke to them in Welsh: '*Dowch
rwan*', which basically means 'Come now'. Well,
you can't expect a sheep to learn a new language
too quickly, so we run around the hills of Durham

speaking Welsh in a Geordie accent! Mind you, back in the day, a lot of Welsh miners came to work in the area where our farm is, so I guess there is some precedent!

We also have Hebrideans on our farm – Nicola's favourite! According to the Hebridean Sheep Society, these are 'an economic and attractive primitive breed' from Scotland, similar to sheep from the North European short-tailed group. They are quite small and 'fine boned, with a black or dark brown wool. Their face and legs are largely free of wool and are covered with glossy black hair.' They have slender legs, small feet and incredible horns on the rams or tups, which can be really large and very dramatic. Notably, the ewes often produce twins, which is handy! Believe it or not, in the mid-1970s Hebrideans were considered an endangered breed, with some farming historians suggesting there were no more than forty or so parkland flocks left (comprising only around three hundred animals).

Our Hebrideans are basically trained on a feed bag – you just stand in a gateway where you want them to go, give a little shake of the feed bag and hey presto! It's dead easy: they will run straight over to you and walk where you want them to. They are well known for being able to live off food with poor energy values, and are also useful for keeping invasive plant species at bay. This is one reason why the Society suggests this breed has a well-earned 'reputation as *the* breed for the management of delicate ecosystems'. Coming from harsher upland areas, Hebrideans are much hardier than the more common domestic breeds of sheep and are perhaps the perfect example of us making our flocks more practical for Mum going forward.

Next up we have Herdwicks, which is a remarkable breed from the Lake District. They seem to go into an almost Zen-like state to cope with any extreme conditions. I sometimes look at them in the freezing weather and it reminds me of when you jump into an ice-cold pool or bath – if you splash and flap about, you get cold very quickly, because your movement is breaking the seal of the warm air between your hairs and your skin. But if you stay really still, that is much more efficient and keeps your

body temperature up. The Herdwicks remind me of that when the weather is cutting in across the valley with its bitterly cold, icy winds; and the more extreme the conditions, the more calm they seem to get.

This hardiness is the key reason why these sheep blossomed in the Lake District. Early settlers there had to find ways that their livestock could survive in the harsh climate, with large areas of exposed, common grazing land on the many fells. Herdwicks were seen as a solution centuries ago, but their name goes back much further – according to herdy.co.uk, 'Herdwyck' comes from the Old Norse Viking language and means 'sheep pasture'. Many livestock historians believe this breed was closely allied to the Viking culture. The earliest flock is recorded in the Lake District way back in AD 1564! One of their most amazing traits is what is known as 'heafing' – this is essentially a homing instinct, where the sheep seem to instinctively know the land they are supposed to graze on. This natural homing sense is even passed on from generation to generation, and is very helpful to Lake District farmers, because some of their farms are so big that they might require a ninety-mile round trip if a sheep was to go astray!

Herdwicks are a very dramatic-looking sheep, with a thick fleece. They have square, powerful legs – their stature is known as having 'good bone'. Some of the tups have horns, some don't and it's interesting to note that the hornless look isn't necessarily passed on to their offspring. For our flock of Herdwicks, we borrowed a tup from a very highly regarded Lake District breeder called Joe Weir, who helped us pick our females.

Finally, we have a flock of Hill Cheviots from the Scottish Borders. These take their name from the dramatic range of border hills that have been farmed with livestock for centuries. The Cheviot Sheep Society traces this breed back to as early as 1370, while later years saw the handsome fleece prove very popular in the area, which was fast gaining a reputation for excellent-quality woollen products. Sir John Sinclair, under whose guidance the British Wool Society was formed in 1791, is credited by many with naming the breed and regarded them as 'the perfect mountain sheep'. They thrive at high altitude and produce really incredible wool, so we were very keen to buy some from an award-winning breeder we know called Willy Thompson – he had plenty of choice, as his farm holds 1,500 ewes on 1,600 acres, spread across three miles!

In the past, we have had a variety of other sheep on the farm: when we first started out, we had beautiful Swaledales, which are the very traditional-looking, hardy sheep with curly horns, a black head and white nose; the head grows greyer with age. They have lovely thick wool with a curly top and are named after the Yorkshire valley of Swaledale. They are also brilliant mums and, like the Herdwicks that we have now, they are more than capable of lambing out on the hills. I love their character and to me they are a classic sheep; I just think they fit in so well. I always really enjoyed working with them as a boy because they were so cool-looking and it's definitely one that I'm keen to return to.

We've also had Mashams (pronounced 'Massam') as well, which take their name from that town in North Yorkshire. They are reasonably big sheep yet have an incredible ability to jump over fences! They have been bred for more than a hundred years on the hills scattered around the north of England, so not very far from our farm. They were originally bred from a Teeswater ram and a Dalebred ewe, both of which are well known for being hardy breeds, which also created some longevity, a strong maternal instinct and a great milking ability into the resulting Mashams. They have these kind of ringlets in the fleece which, if you are not careful, can easily get caught in the vegetation that we have around the farm, and if that happens it can be a nightmare to sort out. They will go into vegetation for shelter but come out peppered with all this sharp gorse and it isn't exactly easy or enjoyable to pull all this prickly and stubborn stuff out of their fleece. On our farm, that added quite a bit of maintenance.

What I find fascinating about having had all these different breeds of sheep on the farm over the years is that each breed has its own characteristics. Within a specific breed, each flock can also behave in a certain way. It's incredibly varied actually, how wily some of them are, how flighty some of them are, and how steady some of them are. Drilling down into each flock, individual sheep have their own personalities, too. You learn which ones are good mothers, and which ones are more difficult to control, so there'll always be a couple in the flock who don't like to do what you want them to! You have to keep an eye out for those ones, because you just know they will go the opposite way to where you want the flock to be. Conversely, there will be more compliant sheep, so you spot those and lead them along, then they help drag the rest of the flock through a gate or whatever. Some sheep are more affectionate than others, and so on . . . these are individual animals and you learn about each one every time you are around them.

There is absolutely no doubt in my mind that sheep remember every job you do with them. Sometimes this works against you – the very worst job with a sheep is putting them in the footbath, because they will avoid water at all costs! Sheep instinctively play 'Follow the leader', so if you have one that doesn't want to go where you want, the rest will always go with it and that takes the flock in the wrong direction. Before you know it, the whole flock will follow that one sheep and it's a nightmare! To help with this and make jobs run a lot more efficiently, we have a 'sheep system'. It consists of a gated corridor, called a 'sheep race', that starts off wide then gets smaller and smaller until the sheep are actually running along it in single file. At that point, it is much easier to get them under control and do what you want with them, such as going into a footbath (or maybe administer medicine or whatever it is you need to do).

The footbath itself is a really carefully monitored treatment that prevents any diseases that are induced by spending time on wet ground. Most farms can get really boggy at times, and if that gets out of control then you get what is called foot rot which, as the name suggests, is not a very nice ailment. A sheep is cloven-hoofed, which means it basically has two toes, between which are parts of the foot that are really sensitive. If they get something stuck in there, it can get infected pretty quickly and that can be disastrous.

A variant of the sheep system is the 'shedding gate'. If, for some reason, you need to separate certain sheep into different pens, you have this gate that lets you filter them into one space or another. We also have an amazing bit of kit known as a 'sheep turner', which does exactly what it says on the tin. The sheep runs into this turner and stops; then you pull a handle and it spins the sheep upside down! That way you can trim their feet and also have a really good look underneath.

The lowland breeds like the Hampshires need a higher level of care and attention. Hardier breeds can cope with more challenges. Generally, the hardier breeds are, by definition, easier to manage, so that is another reason why we have those on the farm now; it is all about lower maintenance. We always aim to leave the sheep to their own devices as much as is appropriate.

The role of sheep in British farming has been changing for hundreds of years, and if you drill down into our little farm, it has changed here, too. It's fascinating that after the Black Death in the fourteenth and fifteenth centuries, there were literally fewer people around, so farmers started to use more highland breeds because they required less labour. In other words, even back then people were buying highland breeds that were lower maintenance, exactly the same as we have done with Mum, but for a slightly different reason!

# 4

# Summer

I love summer on the farm, it's a very welcome time
. . . you soak it up because you absolutely know
that come the wintertime the weather is going to
be brutal, so you cherish every single moment of
summer. The length of the days is so enjoyable
– it's almost like you get two days in one up here,
because it gets light so early . . . and there is nothing
better than the sound of a dawn chorus on our

farm! When all the birds start singing, it is just this incredibly invigorating, energizing natural alarm that wakes you up; you look out of the window and the daylight is illuminating the entire farm. For me, that feeling is just like a magnet, I can't NOT go out and be around the fields. Everything is already up and about, making the most of the day ahead, and I love to join them. I find that very inspirational. The feeling is so special that you almost want to bottle it, so that you can then drink it in for the rest of the year until spring comes round again. Instead, you have to somehow capture it in your mind and in your senses.

Everything is set to 'maximum' during summertime. In some ways, I think of the seasons like a mountain: you've got this climb up to summer and once you get to the summit . . . suddenly . . . BANG! Everything is there, right at its peak (before it tips over the top and drops down into autumn and then you are in the lows of winter again). That sense of hitting those ultimate highs is like a natural celebration that you've got to this point of the year. The farming community has a real feeling of celebration in the summer, too, because there are a lot of fairs and shows, everyone meets up, chats, hears all the news; we sit down to eat outside and catch up with old friends – it's great.

Visually, summer is extremely striking: the colours are all just so *rich*, so vibrant; even the light is so bright and crisp, it's like looking at the world in the most advanced Technicolor. Somehow the farm feels bigger, vast even, I suppose because you can see every nook and cranny; the glorious light is illuminating everything for you.

Summer can be incredibly hot on the farm. Due to the south-facing nature of our location, it can get very, very hot and, because you are quite high, you don't realize how powerful the sun can be, especially if there is a breeze. So sun cream is a necessity! You definitely need hats as well, because you can get sunstroke very quickly, exposed on the hills up here, working away.

When you aren't using energy to stay warm, you can divert that into all the work that needs to be done. The workload doesn't stop just because the sun is shining. Due to the heat, shelter is very import ant, so you'll often see a lot of sheep taking cover underneath the trees. Obviously, making sure all the animals have plenty of fresh, clean drinking water is also vital.

Shearing is one of the key early-summertime jobs, because of the warmer months arriving – a sheep that is too hot will attract flies and that can bring disease and infection. The shearing technique used in modern farming is called the Bowen Technique, developed by the New Zealand farmer Godfrey Bowen in the 1940s and 1950s. The only way I can describe it is like peeling an orange in one go, because you want to get the fleece off in a oner, as opposed to just sort of hacking bits off and everything flying about everywhere.

I am often asked if the sheep are frightened when they are being sheared and my honest opinion is . . . absolutely not. The Bowen Technique helps with that, because you don't start with them on their feet: the first thing you have to do is almost put them on to their backsides, grab their front legs and pull them up against you, so they are sitting upright with their front legs up almost at your waist height and their back legs out underneath them. This way they are never actually on their feet and so they are not able to panic and push or rush and get hurt or frightened. Once a sheep has been sheared for the first time, they are even more relaxed in the future.

Every action that you do when you shear a sheep is called a 'blow' – you take the belly wool off first, and then you go down the chest and up the neck, then you start working your way around, ending up rolling the sheep round on to its side, all the time constantly putting in these blows, working your way along the back and then up the rear of the neck and on to the top. It's almost like a dance with a partner – you keep rolling the sheep round and you always have to move your feet in certain positions to turn the sheep.

It is SO PHYSICAL. When you are not skilled at it, or if you are a little out of practice, it is absolute agony. Talk about a gym workout! I'm happy to get stuck into shearing if needed, but when you are doing hundreds of sheep, you can't do it alone. We get someone to come to the farm to help us, and these people are just incredibly skilled and so physically fit and strong. I love watching them at work – it's mesmerizing. In the old days, hand clippers would limit many farmers to around fifty sheep being sheared a day, but with the advent of mechanical and then electrical shearers, a professional can typically remove the fleece in around two to three minutes – the big commercial farms can sometimes shear as many as three thousand sheep in a day! Godfrey Bowen himself once held the world record after shearing 456 sheep in nine hours; at the time of writing, the world record stands at 731 ewes in nine hours at a farm in Cornwall, by Matt Smith. What an achievement! This was also the first time the record had been broken in the Northern Hemisphere, as competitive shearing is a much bigger pastime in territories such as Australasia. Matt was shearing a sheep every 44.3 seconds!

You typically shear your sheep once a year and send the wool to the wool board, an organization that collects, grades, sells and promotes fleece wool. Unfortunately, the price of fleece in recent times has plummeted so that can be very unrewarding and disheartening for farmers. Way back in history, this was most definitely not the case. Wool was in such demand that whole cities were built on its trade, such as what many regard as Europe's oldest, Knossos. Even some ancient scrolls and tablets record sheep shearing in some detail. According to one research report by the Canepal Project, 'Wool was one of the first textiles to be spun and woven and formed the clothing of the people,' such that by Roman times, British wool was widely renowned and coveted. By the time of the Domesday Book in the late eleventh century, sheep were regarded as by far the dominant farm animal. Wool was one of our medieval economy's most important trades. Wars were often funded through taxes levied on the wool trade, and towns that sold wool were usually the most affluent – in the sixteenth century, wool made up *half* of the total English economy!

For many centuries, sheep were prized first and foremost for their wool, so the breeds that produced high quality and abundant fleeces were most popular. Back then, monasteries were one of the biggest

I started gymnastics when I was six and from then it became a complete obsession of mine . . .

At the age of twelve I scored a perfect ten in the national gymnastics finals. This was my perfect 10 trophy awarded to me by world boxing champion Glenn McCrory.

Gymnastics training at the north-east Centre of Excellence.

One of my gymnastics coaches, Mr Crawford, awarding me a medal at the regional finals.

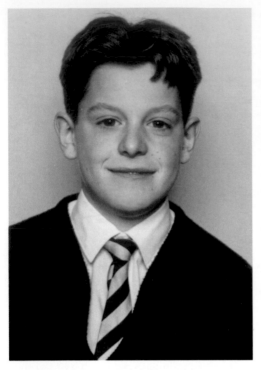

Sporting a centre parting at Belmont Comprehensive school.

My acting class at Queen Margaret's in Edinburgh.

Off to the village fair fancy-dress competition – I was a big fan of the *Incredible Hulk*.

The cast of *Grease* at Durham Sixth Form Centre, the production that changed my career path completely.

A very early driving lesson.

Always building . . .

Moving stone on a Fordson Major.

An early cartoon – the Coco Pops sketch Dad kept in his diary.

My watercolour mallard.

My Kimmeridge Bay squid, painted with its own fossilised ink.

On an episode of *Countryfile* I painted a honey bee sitting on a flower.

While I was in the Atlas Mountains of Morocco, I sketched a mule standing nearby.

The horses at a ploughing match I visited were such a mesmerizing subject I captured them in oils.

Border collies have always been a big part of my life and we've bred a lot of puppies over the years.

Meg, my *Blue Peter* companion. Her triangular ears were her trademark!

Me, Bob and a silkie!

I grew up with horses and they have always had a special place in my heart . . .

One of our favourites, Honey, and her foal Gift.

One of the many horse adventures I've had was playing polo at Ascot.

Grandpa and me on the old Fordson Major.

Malcolm introduced me to vintage tractors — he had the most amazing collection. This is him and me on the Ford 4000 off to the fields.

producers of wool, especially in the north of Eng-land. In years gone by, we were so reliant on wool to make clothes and what have you, and so much care went into making those items, that wool was priced at a premium. However, with the advent of man-made fibres, the appeal of, and demand for, wool has declined. For some farmers this has been finan-cially devastating. Not many people buy a woollen suit these days, but previously that would have been the only choice. It would be wonderful to see wool return to its former popularity.

The problem with wool prices being so low is that farmers still have to shear their sheep for welfare reasons. Of course, wild sheep will moult, so they don't need shearing, but farm flocks need our help.

This means that even if the wool is sold at a loss, the work still has to be done. It is tricky for Mum to make money from her sheep, and the sale of the wool doesn't even cover the cost of the shearing itself. This isn't helped by some of our breeds being a little more complicated to shear – the Hampshires are more expensive to sort out because they have all that lovely facial hair and belly wool.

All of that said, the art of sheep shearing is just a brilliant skill – I find it really exciting and love being involved every summer. If you have never seen this craft in person, I highly recommend finding a farm that is open to the public and going along to watch. It is AMAZING!

Moving from spring into summer, our attention will also start turning to our hay. We are very proud of our ancient hay meadows here on the farm; they are crammed with just the most incredible forage in there, filled with all these herbs and beautiful species that are so rich in nutrients – it is like a magnificent salad! In there you will find species such as harebell, field scabious, vetches, bird's-foot trefoil, yellow rattle (or hay rattle as it is known as well), ox-eye daisy, common spotted orchid, cowslip and red clover, among others. Since we don't use artificial fertilizers and other modern methods to stimulate growth, these meadows have taken years to get to this stage. Nothing is planted, it just develops over time; everything slowly starts to grow and germinate, you just need to have plenty of patience. What an incredible habitat to have on the farm, though; it's a very precious asset.

As a country, we have lost so much ancient hay meadow, largely due to a focus on human food production and, in the process, we have also witnessed a severe decline in so many of these wild flowers. According to the Cumbria Wildlife Trust, the UK has lost a shocking 97 per cent of flower-rich hay

meadows between the 1930s and 1980s due to changes in food production. Regarding this worrying loss of such incredible habitats, that particular trust says, 'Hay meadows are a stunningly beautiful and iconic habitat, which have suffered a serious and rapid decline since the Second World War. At last count, there are now only around 1,000 hectares of upland hay meadows left in the UK.' Drastic action is needed to bring them back and that is something that we are proud to have done on our farm.

Also, as well as our hay meadows creating the most delicious feed, while the flowers are thriving they are supporting a massive invertebrate population – you've got your bees, you've got moths, butterflies, there are hoverflies, they all lay their eggs amongst the leaves, it's a huge destination for tiny insects!

Then the birds come in to feed on the insects, so ground-nesting birds will rummage around in the grass. According to the RSPB, there are up to forty-five species of grasses and flowers per square metre in the best meadows. They provide this entire eco-system. One magical summer experience is to look across a hay meadow that is waist high, because as you do so, you are immersed in all of the pollinators and the sounds of all these insects that live in there. You witness this huge burst of life that happens as you look, it's phenomenal.

We have four upland hay meadows in all. These are cut mid-July/August time. The late cut means that you don't destroy the nesting habitat for certain species of birds. You wait until the ground-nesting birds have raised their young and finished nesting, plus those youngsters will have fledged. Also, by then, all the varied species of flowers and grasses have set their seeds on to the ground. After about a month, we let the sheep graze the new growth of fresh grass known as the 'aftermath'. This does a twofold job, really. The protein-filled new grass builds the ewes up to peak fitness, ready to go to the tups in the autumn, but also their cloven hooves press in all the newly dropped seeds as well as fertilizing the ground as they go! To prevent 'poaching' (when the soil is put under too much pressure) and because the ancient hay meadows are slower growing at a thousand feet up, the sheep are taken off them January/February time and the fields left to flourish till hay time.

There are two different types of food that you can make from a meadow like this: one is silage and the other is hay. You will probably have seen silage on your travels, those big round bales wrapped in black plastic that you come across on the sides of the fields by roads. Before the grass gets to the dry stage, farmers wrap it in these plastic bags and effectively pickle it; the grass ferments in its own juices, a process that keeps a lot of nutrients in there. This tends to be more for cattle than sheep.

We cut the grass and then dry it over a longer period of time. You do this using what's known as a 'Hay Bob' (or hay turner) that goes along and flips the grass over, which exposes the underneath to the sunshine and dries it out; you then go along and do it all again, flipping and drying, until you are satisfied it is ready. This dried grass is then made into square or round bales and put in the hay barn in our yard.

There is a real feeling of harvest and celebration when you get your hay in. I love doing this. That said, it can also be a very anxious time because you are constantly looking at the weather forecast. That's why you see farmers in these months working such long hours. If the weather turns against you, it's usually too late. Sometimes the window of opportunity is very small, so you have no choice but to be out there all day and night. We often have contractors come in who can speed through the process incredibly quickly. Even then there is a gamble, because if you book them too last minute, they will be too busy elsewhere and then you can be in big trouble! If your hay does get wet, you can still use it, but as a rule it just isn't as good. That can be both stressful and expensive, because when that happens you will have to buy hay in. For farms that are not making much – or any – money, that can be a real financial blow. We also pride ourselves on making beautiful hay, so whenever we have to buy stuff in, it feels so disappointing – we don't want to do that unless we absolutely have to.

When you are in the middle of winter and you break open a hay bale, it is magical because instantly you can smell summer. The hay holds this aroma inside incredibly well – it is so emotive and evocative that you are immediately transported back to that summer meadow, which is such a welcome experience when it is freezing cold and dark.

Throughout winter, I am always looking at the soil, all churned up and muddy or maybe swamped in snow and ice, and I think, *How on earth is this going to recover?* But breaking open a bale of hay and smelling summertime reminds you that Mother Nature will fix it; the hay bale is absolute evidence that the damage of winter can be repaired, and it has been so for years and years. All the elements that you love about summer are there in your hands and it gives you hope for the warmer months. I often notice the various species of flowers, crammed into this hay like some beautiful display of pressed flowers, all captured inside the bale, these delicate, beautiful reminders that summer will come again.

One final word about hay – and I recognize that this probably isn't why most farmers get anxious about getting the hay in quickly. Due to my TV work, I am so lucky to be able to live on a farm but simultaneously dip into these amazing TV worlds like I do. This sometimes makes life pretty hectic though – every four years I find myself in a rush to get the hay in, because I usually have to go off to commentate on the Olympics!

At this point, I want to rewind a few years to explain a little bit more about the career path that took me from being a teenage farming lad selling calves at market and competing at national gymnastics to a job presenting on one of the most iconic children's TV shows ever and – eventually – commentating at the Olympics just after getting the hay in!

At the age of sixteen, I went off to Durham Sixth

Form Centre in the city – that was a very formative time in my young life. My form tutor Mr O'Leary was a really energetic character, always cracking jokes, and he was very musical, a great piano player. Most crucially for my future, he was also in charge of the school drama performances.

Towards the end of my first year at sixth form, I joined the cast for his production of *Grease* and I absolutely loved that whole experience. Initially, I was asked to be a stunt double for one of the actors. The idea was that at a certain point, this actor would run off stage, then I would run on in the same outfit and do all these back flips and somersaults then run back off, and nobody would notice there was a body double. That was the plan, anyway. However, during the week leading up to the first night of the production, this actor fell ill with laryngitis and couldn't speak, so because I had been to all the rehearsals, they asked me if I would step in and take his part.

I wasn't sure, so I went home and told my mum and dad and straight away, they were like, 'Give it a go, Matthew!' My dad had done some am-dram when he was younger and he was really enthused; he said to me, 'You'll love it!'

So I went into college the next day and told them I'd give it a go.

My dad was right.

I LOVED IT.

The moment I walked on stage on that first night, I thought, *Oh my God, this is AMAZING!*

The buzz felt very similar to when I was competing in gymnastics. That sport is obviously very physical and technical, but at its heart it's also very much a performance. Likewise, that first night on stage felt right for me, in fact it felt *brilliant*. We even used my dad's old 1946 Dodge, which he often picked me up from school in, and that made the performances feel even more special. (In 2021, much to my dad's delight, we got this wonderful classic car restarted after years of standing silent.)

Performing in *Grease* was something new, it was something exciting, and I loved every minute. Indeed, my experience appearing in *Grease* was so pivotal that I changed my college courses as a result – after the show had finished, the teachers were really kind about my performance and said they felt I should reassess what A Levels I was studying. I had initially been doing Biology, Sports Science (my aim was to be a physio, and ironically, my wife is exactly that!) and Classics, but after *Grease*, I changed the latter for Theatre Studies. I was delighted to make the change – with my dyslexia, I had found some of the subjects very challenging, so to be able to do Theatre Studies instead was a huge boost.

As soon as I had that production of *Grease* under my belt and then changed courses, it felt as if my trajectory changed massively for the better. Suddenly this fairly unexpected series of events was pushing me into the entertainment world that I'm in now.

One time on my Theatre Studies course, we had to perform *A Midsummer Night's Dream*. I was playing Oberon, who is king of the fairies and a man of the woods and what have you. I had this idea to use actual trees on the stage, so we measured everything we needed then went down into our woodlands and gathered up what we could easily and appropriately get our hands on. We crammed all this wood on to a trailer and drove over to the Sixth Form, then spent hours and hours setting up all these branches and trunks on stage. I got some squares of plywood for bases and screwed these various bits of trees to them. Then we put leaves on the floor and my mate lit it all up brilliantly with the stage lights: it looked amazing! I've always hoped that at some point in the future I might replicate the performance in the actual woodlands – albeit without the plywood! – but that hasn't happened yet. Maybe it will one day – you never know!

I worked hard and did OK with my A Levels but my grades weren't quite sufficient to qualify to study for a degree in physiotherapy, so instead – and principally because of what I'd achieved in my gymnastics – I got a place to study Sports Science at Teesside University. I was a little apprehensive, to be honest, as I knew that career path was going to be a long and arduous journey and also my recent discovery of the performing arts had pretty much completely taken me over!

My group of university friends would often go out into Middlesbrough to the various nightclubs. One of our favourite things to do was watch 'Disco Inferno', which was this 1970s re-enactment group up on stage in a nightclub; it was a class night out and we'd be laughing all evening. I started to think that I quite fancied being involved myself, so one evening at the end of the show, after everyone had gone home, I went to see the guy who was in charge. I waited for him at the stage door and, when he appeared, I just came straight out with it.

'How do I go about getting a job with your troupe?'

'Well, what do you mean?'

'I want to try out to be in your group.'

I'm not sure if he was impressed or perhaps just taken aback!

'OK, right,' he said, 'come back next week and we will see how you get on. I will shove you on for a minute or so and see what you are made of.'

'Fantastic.'

I thanked him then started to walk away.

'Make sure you bring a wig and some flares!'

The next day, I walked around all the local charity shops in town rummaging around for 1970s clothes. I'm not sure what the people at the tills thought this eighteen-year-old was doing, asking for flares and loud, wide-collared shirts! Anyway, I eventually found a great wig, some hideous flares and a pair of dazzlingly white slip-on loafers. The wig was blond with lighter highlights and – in the nicest possible way – resembled a Lady Diana hairstyle, so I sort of brushed it into this side parting with a bit of a mullet at the back. I also found some Aviator sunglasses to wear, and put a Velcro strap on the back to stop them flying off when I did my somersaults.

The next week, the manager of the troupe was true to his word and confirmed that he was going to throw me on stage. For my slot, I asked them to play 'Greased Lightning', which I knew really well from my sixth-form performance days. When my turn came, I went up there and was dancing away, really giving it everything, I threw in some backflips and somersaults, I was really going for it! When I had finished, one of the performers came over to me, complete with a full wig and equally enormous flares and said, 'Do me a favour, don't leave the stage!'

I got the job!

I was getting seventy quid a night, too!

I was Butch Vendor, the LA Bar Tender. Other beautifully named characters included Lionel Flare, Richard Itchin and Randy Todger. Part of my act was to juggle bottles behind a cocktail bar. Luckily, my dad has always been very handy with wood-working, so he made me wooden replicas of the bottles – I would start my act by pouring out all these actual cocktails into oversized glasses, then I would switch the real glass bottles for the wooden replica ones underneath the bar top and start all this crazy juggling, and no one was any the wiser! Thanks, Dad!

Luckily, back when I was a kid, I'd always been obsessed with trying daring things out, whether it was juggling or unicycling . . . anything! In fact, the more ludicrous the idea, the more I wanted to try. I actually asked for a unicycle one Christmas and spent weeks out in the freezing cold of the yard, riding round on this one-wheeled contraption. All those years later, that obsession with trying out crazy stuff paid off, because I needed to be juggling every night!

Being in that 1970s troupe was a great time: we travelled widely around the north performing in all these clubs, the crowds were always up for a great time and it was an hilarious bunch of people that I was working with. It was absolute magic, travelling around; we did a club called Pier 39 in Cleethorpes and Hedonism in Barnsley; we did the Empire Middlesbrough, absolutely living the dream. At one show at Cleethorpes, I noticed this beautiful girl in the audience and, for me, it was love at first sight.

My future wife, Nicola, on the other hand, had no idea!

While I was admiring Nicola from the stage, I was obviously dressed in some pretty garish 1970s gear, so it's no surprise that she had no idea of her new admirer! Before the show started, I went over and introduced myself, she told me her name but it was quite a fleeting initial meeting, to be honest, as I had to go and get changed. For the next couple of weeks, I would go over before the show, say hello and have a catch-up but then keep disappearing again! Nicola says she kept wondering if I was going to be there again each week, buy her a drink, have a chat and just vanish again!

Now, one of my pals was playing Richard Itchin, the DJ, and he'd do the most hilarious links in between songs from his booth. I'd been telling him what had been going on with this girl and he said, 'You can't leave it like that!'

That night, we hadn't been on stage that long when

Richard Itchin said, 'Butch would just like to say a big hello to Nicola, who he first met a few weeks ago, and they keep having these magical moments before he disappears off into his disco dream world!'

At this point, Nicola was shocked to say the least, it was so ridiculous. I was standing there awkwardly adjusting my sunglasses and slapping my side-parting while grinning self-consciously through my whitened teeth. After the show, I went over and spoke to Nicola properly, but I had no idea which way it was going to go!

Thankfully, she agreed to go out with me on a date.

Our first date was a day trip to Lincoln. At the time, my late grandpa lived very near the Humber Bridge and I would stay with my grandparents every week for this leg of the disco tour. I loved stopping with them and we always had a ball! When I told him I wanted to take this girl out, I asked him where I should take her. He said, 'Lincoln is lovely.'

With the money I'd earned from Disco Inferno, I'd saved up and bought this silver-blue Renault 19; it looked like a sales rep's car and I was really proud of buying it myself. I spent £2,400 on it, even though it wasn't really a young lad's car at all. One day, I was driving back to the farm on a country road that was on a really steep incline when, all of a sudden, the bracket on the back of the driver's seat broke, the seat flew back and suddenly I was looking at the ceiling of the car as I was driving along! I had to grab the steering wheel and pull myself back up to avoid careering off the road. I have no idea how I didn't have an accident.

I somehow got back to the farm and wedged a piece of wood into the bracket, so that it would be safe to drive, then I got myself to my grandparents where my gran Sheila put a kitchen stool in between the driver's seat and the back seat. I drove round for weeks with this stool behind the seat to stop it from dropping down.

Anyway, for my first date with Nicola, I picked her up in my Renault 19 and asked her, 'Where do you want to go?'

'I don't mind,' she said.

At this point, I got my AA map out (I love a good map) and, pretending to be spontaneous, I said, 'What about Lincoln, I wonder what that's like?'

So that's where we went. By this point, given she'd mostly seen me in 1970s flares and a wig, I knew she must like me because she was still there! We went to a place Grandpa had recommended for lunch, but Nicola was too nervous to eat. I munched my way through a jacket potato while she just sat there watching me eat! After that, we had a lovely walk up the hills, and we got on famously.

We've been together ever since.

Lincoln . . . good shout, Grandpa.

Me and Nicola used to go off on crazy day trips together and we would always be playing 1970s music in the car as well. We'd drive to a town, then spend the day rifling through charity shops for gear from that decade, too – flares, wigs, all that – then I'd wear them on the show that night. I'd always drive her home in the early hours of the morning and make sure she got back safely, but at first I don't think her mum was too impressed when I sometimes went in for a cup of tea. To be fair, all she'd heard was that I was some kind of 'nightclub dancer' . . . and I often still had the teeth whitener on!

Eventually, Nicola's mum actually came to watch the show because my relationship with her daughter was getting more serious. That was so weird, knowing her mum was in the crowd, watching. Her mum seemed a lot happier after that; she realized the show was just fun and games.

Nicola is not a townie; she was from a village, but she had never really had anything to do with animals other than the cat that she grew up with. When she came to the farm for the first time she was quite nervous of dogs, and our dogs were going nuts, which startled her quite a bit! She coped brilliantly and started to fall in love with our farm and way of life really quickly and threw herself into it wholeheartedly. It was a real joy for me to start showing Nicola all the things that I had grown up with and for her to be seeing it all for the first time; to watch her falling in love with the place as a young woman was wonderful. Nicola has that rare combination of being both very academic but also incredibly practical, so she was a natural around the farm. She is not one for preening herself or being obsessed with fashion and all that kind of stuff; instead, she loves to be as mucky and as muddy as me; she will always roll her sleeves up and immerse herself in whatever job needs doing.

Back in those early days, I used to go round and work on her mum's garden, do the veg beds, mow the lawn, just generally be useful, and I think that helped my cause . . . eventually she realized that there was more to me than just a wig and some flares!

I'd been feeling for some time that the whole Sports Science career and degree at Teesside wasn't for me. I knew it was going to take forever and I just wasn't convinced my heart was in it as much as it should be; there was this growing sense that academically it was going to be too much for me. Conversely, I kept coming back to my love of drama and being on stage. My teachers were always going on about going to a drama school and I was just fascinated, so in the end I went home one day and talked to my parents about the idea of switching courses.

I vividly remember sitting in the lounge, we had the fire on and I wasn't entirely sure how I would broach the subject or indeed how they might react. Mum and Dad had always supported me in everything that I'd ever wanted to do, they had always been right behind me, they had only ever helped me get to where I wanted to be – but even so, I was worried about what they were going to say if I told them I wanted to stop doing all the sports science stuff and change to drama – which is, of course, a much less conventional route to take.

Calmly, albeit nervously, I explained what I was thinking, that I wanted to give drama a real go and stop the sports science.

'Well, Matthew,' said my dad, grinning, 'I am over the moon!'

Mum was the same. 'I am delighted!'

They were both so excited for me.

What amazing parents they are.

We talked and talked and it was really exciting: they just told me to go for it, work hard and try my very best, like they'd always taught me. I was so, so pleased, I can't tell you. Looking back at the way they had always supported me, I shouldn't really have been surprised by their reaction at all. And what with Dad's own background in am-dram, I should've guessed. However, as a teenage lad telling his parents he wanted to change course so dramatically, there was always going to be a seed of apprehension.

No need.

'Go for it, Matthew!'

With a real spring in my step, I went back to see my drama teacher, Miss Lennon, at Durham Sixth Form Centre and said, 'Right, what do I need to do to get into a drama school and how does this all work?' She helped me figure out all the monologues I needed for admissions auditions and how to prepare myself for the process. I ended up playing Caliban, 'a feral, sullen, misshapen creature' in Shakespeare's *The Tempest*. That was a really physical piece of theatre to attempt, I was literally in all these auditions upside down and back flipping while delivering Shakespeare lines. I think, looking back, it was all quite experimental!

Long story short, after auditioning at a number of drama schools, I was offered a place at Queen Margaret's in Edinburgh. That wasn't too far from the farm, just about ninety minutes over the Scottish border in my Renault 19. That meant I could go home at weekends if I wanted to and help out on the farm. It seemed like the perfect option.

At this point, I should admit that because of my dyslexia, I had never read an entire book. So, turning up at Queen Margaret's was pretty daunting, to be perfectly honest. What I used to do was go to the city library and take out all our coursework titles as audio books; they also had many of the plays recorded and even quite a few on video.

I'd known for ages that Nicola was the girl that I wanted to marry. We were young but had soon talked about getting engaged. She was studying at Nottingham University at the time and I couldn't think of anywhere more perfect than the Major Oak in Sherwood Forest (the biggest oak tree in Britain) to ask her to marry me.

My sister was a jeweller at the time and offered to make me a ring on my student budget, which she did beautifully. I travelled down from drama school in Edinburgh to Nicola's physio school in Nottingham for the weekend and we went off to Sherwood Forest for the day. I remember feeling really nervous and strangely not quite myself.

I was getting more and more flushed as we got closer to the Major Oak. I looked up ahead and thought, *Why don't I just do it now, just in case there's loads of tourists when we get there?* I've often lived by the mantra 'There is no time like the present', so instead of waiting to get to the biggest oak in Britain, I decided to ask her on a small, woodland path. To this day, I still don't know what she thought: if she was anticipating me asking, or if it came totally out of the blue. I just dropped down on one knee, pulled out the ring and asked her to marry me. She said yes without hesitation! I'd had to guess the size of her finger and the ring was a little bit big, so after calling all our family and friends from a phone box, we drove to a jeweller's to get a plastic loop that fastened to the back of the ring, to stop it slipping off her finger. I didn't want anyone else to resize it other than my sister. We then went out for a Mexican meal to celebrate. It was a place with student discount and you could take your own wine which, along with the spice, was causing me to have yet more hot flushes.

Leaving each other was always difficult, but I travelled back to Edinburgh *elated*. I couldn't work out if I was giddy from the experience or hung-over from the alcohol, but I was boiling hot. It turned out that for the whole weekend I'd been experiencing the onset of glandular fever, so on arrival back in Edinburgh, I ended up spending the next three weeks in bed, 270 miles away from my new fiancée!

Life was going really well for me in Edinburgh, there was a brilliant bunch of people that I was with and we had an absolute ball. I loved it. The first year was a blast and student life was just getting better and better.

Then one day in 1999, a few months into my second year, Nicola's aunty phoned her up, unexpectedly.

'Nicola, I've seen a magazine article saying the BBC is looking for a new presenter for *Blue Peter.*'

'Right . . .' said Nicola, slightly bemused at first.

'That would be amazing for Matthew.'

Nicola called and told me what her aunty had said.

'Matthew, this would be brilliant for you. You're perfect for this. What do you think?'

'Wow, OK, well, what do you think?' I asked.

'I think you should give it a go,' Nicola said. Just like my mum and dad had said when I was first asked to do the part in *Grease*.

'Do you know what, Nicola? I think I will.'

I never said anything to the teaching staff at Queen Margaret's because officially you were not really supposed to go off and do anything until you were fully trained. I was only just over a year into a three-year course but that didn't put me off. I thought, *I know, I'll phone up the BBC and just see what the situation is*. I watched some episodes of *Blue Peter* and spotted that at the end of the credits, there was a man called Steve Hocking listed as 'Editor'.

*He must be in charge*, I figured.

Obviously this is way before smartphones, so with his name in mind, I called Directory Enquiries and said, 'Can you give me the number for the BBC, please?'

It seems almost comical to believe now, but armed with only a general switchboard number, I literally rang up the BBC Television Centre in London and said, 'Oh, hello, can you put me through to Steve Hocking, please?'

Amazingly, they put me through to his office, and his secretary answered. She must've wondered who on earth was on the other end of the phone.

'Hello, I wonder if you could help me, please? I'm trying to get through to Steve Hocking.'

'Er, he's a bit busy at the moment. Who is calling, please?'

'My name is Matt Baker . . . don't worry, I will call back in ten minutes.'

I put the phone down, waited, then called back ten minutes later.

Steve was still 'busy', so I called back again a while later.

'Can I ask what exactly it is regarding, please?' his secretary asked (understandably) after I'd called the third time.

'I think I'm the next *Blue Peter* presenter.'

'Ah, well, I will stop you there, I'm afraid, because

we've already been through a very long selection process and we are nearly decided.'

I just went for it.

'OK, so you're not going to give me a chance, then?'

I could almost hear her thinking, *I don't know, am I going to give you a chance?*

I kept going.

'What would I have had to have done to get to this point?'

'Er, well, you would have had to send a showreel in.'

'Right, what's a showreel?'

She patiently explained that it was a video of all the things that I had done in the past.

'OK, so you're saying if I send you a showreel over the next few days, then you will have a look?'

'Er, yes, I think so.'

'Great, thanks, I will be back in touch really soon . . .'

I put the phone down and shouted, 'Dad! Get the video camera ready, we're making this thing called a showreel!'

The video that I sent in a couple of days later was the most random collection of things I'm sure they've ever seen at the BBC, all filmed by my dad. In fact, the first thing you actually hear is not me at all, but Dad shouting, 'I'm ready!' Then I appear on a quad bike welcoming everyone to the farm. We were lambing at the time and I thought, *The townies will love this* . . . We filmed me lambing a sheep. I was chatting to the camera about all the young animals, how that all worked; then we went off and I started unicycling around the courtyard! I explained all about the wildlife in the hedgerows, and then I did a guided tour around the ancient woodland and did some somersaults off the hay bales! I said I was a professional dancer – maybe not strictly true, but I was being paid seventy pounds a night by Disco Inferno, remember!

I posted the VHS tape off to the BBC and waited.

Two days later the phone rang.

It was a London number.

'Hello, Matthew, it's Claire from the *Blue Peter* office.'

'Claire! Hello! Have you seen my video?'

'Oh yes, Matt, I have. In fact, we've ALL seen that video!'

'I'm sorry it isn't professionally shot, I haven't really done anything like that in the past, so it was just my dad and his camera . . .'

'Yes, we could tell. Anyway, Matt, listen, what are you doing the day after tomorrow?'

\*

I'd never been to London before so I went down there with Dad and that was a big culture shock. It's not like the Dales! We made our way to the TV Centre in Wood Lane, just up from Shepherd's Bush, and I clearly remember walking out of White City Tube Station; then, shortly after, there was this building that I'd seen on Saturday morning kids TV throughout my childhood, suddenly in front of me in all its glory.

As I walked up to the gates, I turned to my dad and said, 'Dad, I'm nervous, I don't know what to say to these people.' It felt like a massive moment in my life. I'd somehow got myself into this scenario but it was suddenly pretty daunting.

It was just like being on the top of the high bar, thinking, *Right, you are going to let go . . . are you going to catch it or are you going to land on your head?*

Dad said, 'Matthew, listen: don't say anything that's not true and most importantly of all . . . just be yourself.'

Steve Hocking, the editor that I had researched when I first phoned the *Blue Peter* office, was waiting for me when I got into the room. After saying hello, he said that everyone in the office had been watching me unicycling around the farm and somersaulting off bales of hay.

'Is that all real, Matt?'

'Er, yes, it is. I live a pretty random life on our farm!'

Then he said, 'OK, can I ask you, what news-papers do you read and what have you seen recently on *Blue Peter* that you would have liked to have done?'

'OK, so, I don't read any papers and, as for the show, well, to be honest with you, Steve, I don't think your dogs are trained very well . . . so I would love to train your dogs. I love training sheepdogs and ours on the farm can do a lot more than sit on a sofa.'

Steve obviously didn't mind me saying this, because we had a really enjoyable chat and I thought it had gone pretty well, but of course you never know. I eventually made my way out of the BBC and met up with my dad, who was waiting near the entrance.

'How did it go, son?' he said as we started to walk off towards the Tube.

'OK, I think. I did what you said – I was myself.'

Dad put his arm around my shoulder and said . . .

'Perfect.'

Not long after that trip with my dad, the *Blue Peter* team contacted me and said, 'We have five potential presenters already that we really like, but we want to put you in as a wild card, so we would like you to formally audition.'

It was all moving very fast now!

They wanted to send me a script by fax which seemed incredibly hi-tech at the time, but in classic Durham Dales style, we didn't have a fax machine at the farm. So, we actually went out and bought one, just to receive that script and for *Blue Peter* to get in touch!

This fax of this script was basically a version of one of the shows that they were going to do that week. There was what they called a 'make' in there, too, which is the famous *Blue Peter* feature where the presenters make something on screen (often accompanied by the iconic TV line, 'Here's one I made earlier . . .'). They wanted us to make a Christmas card in the audition, which suited me down to the ground, because as you know I love my art, so I started practising how to make this festive card. I got the ironing board out in the kitchen and all this different coloured card from our craft box that we kept upstairs, then I made loads of these cards. However, it dawned on me that I needed to make them upside down and back to front while *looking towards where a camera would be.* Maybe it was the gymnastics background, but I just repeated making this process over and over, so I knew that on the day it would feel like second nature.

In the fax from the BBC it also said that 'We want you to interview someone while bouncing on a trampoline.'

Now, I suspect for most of the hopefuls in the audition process, this was possibly the worst news, but for me – wow – I was delighted. Bring it on!

I travelled back down to London for the audition. Before that started, we watched the show go out live, the idea being to see who could then follow on in a style that would work. All the audition hopefuls were waiting in different rooms, expectantly, but we kept passing each other in the corridor. I don't remember much about the other people, although I can remember one guy: he was wearing this thick, fleecy, Aran jumper – although that might be a very niche thing that only a farmer would notice.

Then I found out that we would also be reading from an autocue.

That really panicked me. This was very new to all of us, obviously, but for me, with my dyslexia, this was a major obstacle.

*Oh my God, this is going to be a nightmare!*

I'd prepared with the script in tiny detail but this autocue threw me off, so when it came to my turn to audition I just fell back on my photographic memory of the script and then freestyled . . . I knew what I was supposed to be saying, but I delivered it in a way that didn't rely on the autocue – because, to be honest, I couldn't read what was on there. I started relaxing and threw in a few little jokes, a handful of personal little phrases, just as a kind of deflection tactic really. I then suddenly realized that the crew were all smiling, which in turn boosted my confidence and made me relax even more.

On reflection, having presented shows on TV for years since then, I now know that by freestyling and avoiding the autocue, I allowed my personality to come to the surface, avoided sounding wooden and also set myself apart from the other candidates. At the time, I wasn't thinking that, I was just trying to dig myself out of a hole with the autocue. There was a big, long spiel about the *Blue Peter* Appeal which was quite complicated (I remember a few tongue-twisters in that), then I did the 'make' with the Christmas cards which went really well and, overall, I felt good.

Next up was the interview on the trampoline, which was designed to gauge how well you could interview someone in a challenging situation. Never mind the autocue, I was still slightly over-awed by the TV studio: it was massive and there were hundreds of lights and cameras everywhere; I'd never seen anything like that before. However, when I walked into the studio, one of the first faces I saw was a really lovely lady that I knew from the gymnastics world in Lilleshall – happy days!

As soon as I got on the trampoline, I was totally in my element. I was bouncing around, chatting away to the production crew about what they needed me to do; it was great fun. I figured out where the cameras were and spotted the red lights on the top of the ones that were recording, so I got my bearings while I was bouncing up and down, getting warmed up.

They literally couldn't have picked a better test for me – that trampoline was such a release. Having felt so pent up with the dreaded autocue, now I could be totally free. I was bouncing and somersaulting higher and higher, firing off all these questions, cracking jokes and loving every second. Back in my gymnastics days, I was used to talking with all my coaches while I was upside down, so for me it felt so liberating to actually be doing that as part of an audition and I felt so grateful that I had this opportunity to show them what I could do.

What did worry me was that I felt I tripped over my words in certain parts of my earlier audition, so despite the trampoline element going well, I was worried I just wasn't going to be suitable for what they needed. I was convinced I had messed up.

Literally a couple of days later, the phone rang again.

The same London number.

The same lady from the *Blue Peter* office, asking me to go back to the BBC. Initially, I thought, *Blimey, that's a long way to go again!* so I asked her, 'Is it going to be good news?'

'It's really good news, Matt.'

So that was how I got my job on one of Britain's most-loved children's TV shows. From the time that Nicola's aunty called and said she'd seen a magazine article with the news that the previous presenter was leaving to getting the job was just over one month.

Now all I had to do was go to drama school and tell them I was leaving, and I wasn't sure how they might react.

'Er, I won't be coming into college any more, I'm afraid.'

'Oh, why?' asked the tutor, slightly suspicious, given my reputation as a bit of a prankster.

'Er, because I've got a job presenting *Blue Peter*.'

'Ah, yes . . . of course you have, Matt, of course you have!'


You might think that all this *Blue Peter* and London media world seems a long way away from our farm in the Durham Dales . . . and you'd be right. In summertime, I was used to shearing and getting the hay in, not reading scripts and talking to TV producers.

I'm not going to pretend that I dived into the life of a TV presenter and was immediately at home. It was 1999 and I was only just twenty-one. In a heartbeat, my life had turned around. Within a few days, instead of waking up and looking out across the valley from our beautiful farm, I was in the car, with my belongings shoved in a bag, heading down the M1 to the capital city.

Talk about a baptism of fire!

Going down to the city was a MASSIVE eye-opener, an almighty 'culture shock'. My instant reaction was, *Oh my gosh, this is too full on!* The amount of people, the hectic tempo, *the lack of greenery*, the pollution – as the crow flies, London is about 250 miles from where I lived, but it might as well have been a million.

The first thing I did was go to an estate agent to find somewhere to stay. This chap in a pinstriped suit asked me what sort of place I was looking for, but he didn't seem to have too many farmhouses for rent and there was a distinct lack of any land for livestock.

'All I really need is somewhere with some trees.'

'Brilliant, I've got the PERFECT place!' he said.

He drove me to Chiswick High Road to see a small flat on the main road.

'Here you go,' he said as we parked up. 'You won't find anywhere better than this,' then pointing to an old, very tired stump of a sycamore sticking out of some wonky, broken slabs in the pavement, '. . . and look,' he said, 'a tree.'

\*

The very first time I was ever in a live TV studio was on 25 June 1999. I remember the date precisely because it was also when I was introduced on air as *Blue Peter*'s twenty-eighth presenter! Nobody actually gave me a 'guided tour', I was literally thrown in at the deep end and suddenly I was on national telly. They asked me to introduce myself, so I kept it simple, 'Hello, my name's Matt Baker and I'm from Durham.' It was at that moment that I suddenly realized, *Crikey, I'm actually doing this now, this is real!*

That night, I went back to my flat in Chiswick on my own and was at a bit of a loose end, because I didn't really know what to do with myself of an evening and I didn't know anybody in the city. I walked to the pub down the road and as I stood at the bar, these four blokes in the corner were looking across and one of them shouted, 'Here he is, *Blue Peter*, here's one I made earlier . . .'

*OK, so this is going to be a bit of a change!*

The first few shows seemed to go well and the team were all really nice. It wasn't until about a month into my job on the show that one of the ladies realized I hadn't been shown around the studio – she was very sweet and actually took me by the hand and said, 'So this is a camera . . .' and I thought, *Yes, I have kind of worked that one out by now!*

I'm not going to lie, I didn't like London at all

when I first got there. When you leave somewhere like our farm and head down south to the bright lights of the city, the BBC, *Blue Peter* and what have you . . . well, obviously it is a world away from waking up early listening to the birds, walking round the woodlands or feeding all the animals in the cold, crisp and clean air. I didn't realize what I was going to miss and how I was going to feel when those parts of my life suddenly weren't there. I missed just wandering out to feed some animals; I missed hearing the birds, seeing the clear sky, smelling the grass . . . there were a million gaps that I couldn't fill by living in London. I was shocked by just how much I missed the farm and that was pretty hard to deal with, to be honest. There I was, on a high street in west London, thinking, *Hang on a minute, what's going on here?*

It wasn't just missing the farm and countryside that was an issue – London living freaked me out at first. Around the Durham villages, you jump on the bus, sit next to someone and have a good chat with them; there's probably only two of you on the bus, so you sit next to each other and have a bit of banter about what's going on.

The first time I got on the Tube, the carriage was empty apart from one woman, so I went and sat two seats down from this lady, turned to her and said,

'Hello, how are you doing today? What you been up to?' She took one look at me, puzzled (and obviously unsettled), then stood up and went to sit down the opposite end of the carriage.

*OK, so this is not like Durham!*

London just felt alien to me. I get that city life has a different energy, that people thrive and get excited by the 'buzz'. I totally get that. But that's not an energy I was used to – I think that nature has a pace and an energy that you can tap into when you are surrounded by it, walking around the countryside, soaking it all in. I'd known nothing else throughout my childhood, so to suddenly switch to a world that was the polar opposite just didn't sit well with me. I didn't feel at ease.

So, although my job on *Blue Peter* was exciting and I was loving every minute, after a few months I decided I had to get out of the city and find some greenery. I'd already started driving out of London at the weekend, just to find some green spaces. Not long after, I found this little cottage in a place called Chalfont St Giles, which was about an hour down the A40. It was next to a big house with a paddock and stables and was up for rent. Nicola was just finishing up with her physiotherapy studies at Nottingham and then she moved to be with me and began looking for work down south. So we started to rent this little house, and I asked the lady who owned the big house what she was doing with the land and she explained that she used to have horses but didn't really know what to do with it now.

'Would you mind if I put some sheep on it?'

A few days later, I found some lovely Oxford Downs (very similar to Hampshires), which were owned by a guy keeping them at the Chiltern Open Air Museum. One thing led to another and he brought a small flock over. I was so happy when all this started happening because that feeling inside of me, that need to be on a farm, to be in nature, was finally being satiated again. I would sort out the sheep early each morning, then go into the BBC for the show.

I need to have that fix of nature every day, as much as I possibly can. I like to exist within the pace of nature, I like to react to the seasons, and I like to be surrounded by and involved in the weather – that flow is something that I like to be a part of. I like to be in tune with what's happening at any given time of the year, whether that's the wildlife migrating or the new arrivals or the harsh winter months . . . whatever nature is doing, I like to be in tune with and react to that. I like to lift up stones and see what is living underneath and, of course, depending on which season you are in, everything can be different from week to week.

For me, as a Durham farming lad, the problem with living in a city is that the seasons are largely invisible. Of course, you still get heavy rain or cold or snow, but the nuances of each season – the details, the smells, sounds, colours – they just aren't there in a city. They are sterilized by the noise, pollution, busyness and concrete. Workers sweep up the leaves and clear away the snow. On many days, you can't even see the sky or the stars. And you really don't want to go lifting up too many rocks in a city! I like to look out of the window to predict the weather forecast, not see it on a screen and be told by somebody else what an app says.

Sometimes people in cities say to me that they spend most of their time sheltering from the weather; maybe it's too cold, wet, windy – or hot, even. I don't see it like that up on our farm – in my opinion, there's no such thing as bad weather, just the wrong choice of clothing.

I missed looking across the valley and seeing the weather coming in. You can guess how long you have until the rain starts or the sunshine returns. Years of living outdoors as well as learning from people who know best have taught me there are so many signs of what the weather is going to do next. For example, when it is about to rain, you get a very obvious change in the humidity. It is almost like you feel it in your ears – you become this human barometer and sense the atmospheric pressure change. You know change is coming: it gets more and more intense; it starts quite dull and it's almost like this wave effect. You then look up to the clouds as they roll in; there are different cloud levels that you look at. The high-level cloud will tell you which direction the wind is travelling, so you watch the clouds, you feel the air pressure and then you will *know*. You can pretty much feel it within two or three minutes of when it will start raining. You can't really tell when it will finish, but you can definitely tell when it will start – and you'll start to smell the equivalent of a dew-filled morning.

In case you look up and think, *A cloud's a cloud, right?* – well, it can get way more complicated than that! The World Meteorological Organization categorizes ten main 'genera' of clouds, divided into three levels – low, middle and high, depending on which part of the atmosphere they are usually found in. Above 16,500 feet you will see the layer that you fly above in an aeroplane, such as cirrus, cirrocumulus and cirrostratus clouds; the medium range is above 6,500 feet, but it is the low clouds that we will most often see nearest to us, below this point. This includes clouds whose names many of us are familiar with, such as cumulus and cumulonimbus.

All the names of clouds originate from Latin, and have some fascinating meanings – for example, *cumulus* denotes 'heaped up/puffy, cauliflower-like', while *cirrus* means 'high up and wispy'. Any cloud with the word *nimbus* attached is classed as rain-bearing and these are the ones to keep an eye out for!

I like to react to life. I don't want to be sheltered from what might happen next. I enjoy the experience; I want to feel the challenges and be in the middle of it all happening. Sometimes that might mean you get battered by unexpected changes but even then, when you are really feeling exposed, at least you are still *living* and experiencing what life has to throw at you.

So many people don't even see the seasons and that is such a shame; they are missing out on so much. It's not about moaning that it's cold, it's about *celebrating* the cold, it's about knowing *why* it's cold, it's about knowing what the plants and animals will do *because* it's cold; it's feeling that chill and knowing that our trees will go into lockdown so that they can get their fuel and be ready to burst into life again in spring. So many people only know it's cold because their smartphone tells them it is. Or they notice the frost because their car needs scraping. If any of this sounds familiar, then I am excited for you to discover more about nature around you. Otherwise you are only limiting yourself. Give yourself those opportunities to experience nature and, I promise, you will be happier throughout your day.

# 5

# Horses

I grew up with horses. One of my favourites was a horse called Honey that my mum rescued. There used to be schemes where you could effectively rent a horse for the summer and my mum had always wanted to have one, but cost was an issue. Anyway, Mum rented this one particular horse called Honey but when she arrived she was, sadly, in a very poor state: she had saddle sores and numerous scarred patches of bad skin, etc. My parents were really upset and – long story short – they refused to send the horse back. Eventually, they managed to buy her and keep her.

Honey was a chestnut mare with a white blaze down the front of her face and a beautiful soft pink nose with grey lips. She was a beauty, standing 15.2 hands up to her withers (shoulders). A hand is a measurement that is, literally, the width of your hand including the thumb – an ancient unit of length which was eventually standardized at four inches (10.16 centimetres). The unit was originally defined as 'the breadth of the palm including the thumb' and, in case you are thinking people have different size hands, it was actually a statute of King Henry VIII of England that was used to establish the width of a hand at four inches.

When I was about six, I started lessons at a place called Penshaw Monument, which is an amazing columned Roman building. I rode a feisty little pony called Shandy, so characterful, and I really enjoyed spending time at the riding school. This pony loved to gallop and that got me very quickly used to the speed that horses travel at. Basically, the four speeds of your horse are the walk, the trot, the canter and the gallop. You also quickly learn that some horses and ponies miss that trot phase, and launch straight into a canter/gallop and you are off! Well, Shandy used to go off like a rocket – one time I remember galloping up to Penshaw Monument thinking, *I'm going to get there long before everybody else!* I arrived ages before the others, so I then had to spend an anxious few minutes waiting for everyone else to join me, as I didn't want to be left alone with this pony for longer than I needed to. She was a cheeky little character!

Eventually, I grew enough physically and gained enough experience that I was able to ride Honey; I loved that gentle old horse. She was quite a size for me to jump on as a young lad, but I was never frightened – she had such a lovely temperament.

One day my mum saw a competition that owners could enter and the prize was your horse being served by a top-class Hanoverian eventing horse at a top stables in North Yorkshire. We went in for this competition and Honey won! We took Honey up to the stables to meet this stallion, and it was on a very, *very* steep hill, so it was pretty hair-raising to get the trailer up there!

For Honey to have gone from such a challenging, difficult background to being a winner who was then served by this elite stallion was just brilliant. When the foal arrived, we called him Gift, as that's what the new arrival felt like as a part of that whole experience.

Honey was a beautifully natured horse. I remember how soft her nose was; she always used to nuzzle into me so closely and push my hands up to see if I had a treat in there for her. Although she was a big old horse, I never felt frightened when I went into her stable – I never, ever felt like she would do anything to hurt me. I loved to just go and stand in her stable and pat her neck; when you are right in close to a horse, it often puts its neck around you and gives a really good hug back. After we lost her, we had her image engraved in a block of granite and placed on a stable door, because she always used to look over the top at us. Such a calm-natured horse, I loved to spend time with her.

I've been lucky to have many wonderful experiences with horses over the years, often in far-flung countries as a result of my TV work. Whenever I am around horses, I think back to when I travelled to the Colorado River in the Grand Canyon and met up with members of the Hualapai Tribe. The name Hualapai means 'People of the tall pines', and their reservation is about one million acres along 108 miles of the Grand Canyon and Colorado River, with the tribe itself amounting to around 2,300 people.

They have deep and very proud traditions, and life on their reservation is rich in hunting, fishing and river rafting. Suffice to say, their relationship with animals is incredibly close and, with regard to horses, they are just awesome to watch at work. They have very spiritual views on animals, which date back centuries, and the spirit of the horse is something they are acutely tuned into. Although I come from a very different background, I can totally relate to that spiritual aura of horses. Being in their presence is calming, relaxing and life-enriching.

Another wonderful experience I've had with these amazing animals was in Outer Mongolia, of all places, quite some way from the Durham Dales. We did a big old Children in Need adventure called *Around the World in 80 Days*, where a number of TV faces re-enacted the famous globe-trotting exploits of Phileas Fogg in the 1872 novel of the same name. Each episode saw a pair of celebrities travel one section of the eighty-day journey, with the aim being to create this relay race around the world. Myself and my great friend Julia Bradbury went on the Trans-Siberian Express for our leg of that project, heading towards our destination which was, as I said, Outer Mongolia . . . just unbelievable. I ended up riding with the local farmers, galloping through this stunning landscape; it was just fantastic. We didn't speak any of the same languages but we were able to communicate and warm to each other through the horses (I am talking about the Mongolian farmers here, not Julia Bradbury). There was a synergy that I would experience on many more occasions to come . . .

A really special moment with horses a little closer to home came one time on Holkham beach in Norfolk, where we took the horses from the Queen's Household Cavalry off on holiday! They taught me how to swim with these horses, and it was amazing. The whole experience was bareback, which was incredible. You walked them down to the water's edge and had to make sure that you were never sideways on, because a big wave might knock them – and you – over. You keep walking them on, out directly towards the horizon, and then suddenly, as it gets deeper and deeper, the horses start to gallop under you, because that's how they swim. At that point, you swing your legs up so your feet are up on their backs, with your arms wrapped around their neck, and in a heartbeat, they are swimming in the sea. What a feeling it is, and the horses love it.

I really do love riding; there is no feeling like it: being up at such a great height, observing the countryside with a magnificent horse – it really is beautiful. My experiences with horses have usually been fabulous, but I must admit to a couple that were less than ideal. Firstly, let me tell you about when I signed up for one of the most bizarre and potentially risky celebrity Sport Relief challenges ever, namely a show-jumping competition called *Only Fools on Horses*! Someone had decided it would be a great idea to get a load of celebrities and famous faces off the telly and film a horse-jumping competition.

The show was aired in July 2006 with the idea that each of the twelve celebrities had to jump for survival every night – along with me 'for the ride' were people such as Jenni Falconer, Nicki Chapman, Ruby Wax, Sara Cox, Paul Nicholas and Sally Gunnell, among others. My horse was called Peter and he was a nine-year-old, standing at 16.2 hands. There were some really tricky equestrian tasks and it was very demanding. Poor Ruby Wax, she took such a battering, she was black and blue from bruises, but kept going; she was stoic, to say the least.

All the competitors lived in this converted stable yard and were taught by really good coaches, such as the late Tim Stockdale; he was one hell of a horse-man – unbelievable. Consequently, we had a fantastic camaraderie and sense of 'team' within the camp; yes, it was a competition but we were all rooting for each other.

Most of us on the show suffered some sort of injury; I managed to dislocate my shoulder one day when I got the pace for a jump all wrong. I'd actually been feeling a growing sense of confidence, I had a lovely connection with my horse, I understood what the instructors were telling me and I was getting better all the time.

*I like this show-jumping lark, this is the thing for me!*

Of course, next thing I did was approach a jump at the wrong pace, which meant the horse got too close to the barrier, he slammed his anchors on and, as he did so, he lifted his head up sharply. The problem was, I was obviously leaning forward in the saddle, getting ready for the jump, so his strong muscular neck met my upper torso and literally popped my shoulder out, so I was riding around with my shoulder hanging out. Luckily, we were able to pop it back in but blimey, that hurt. I sank a few beers that night, for medicinal purposes, of course. Mind you, most of us did! We were like some camp full of walking wounded. Jenni Falconer won the final and, despite all the risks and injuries, the show actually raised £250,000 for Sport Relief, which was something that we were all very proud of.

A second experience with horses that was less than ideal was in April 2009, just after I had started presenting *Countryfile* (which I will come to later) when it moved to an evening slot – in many ways, a dream job for this particular Durham Dales lad!

— and one day we were filming a piece about the rehabilitation of racehorses. It was a really interesting subject. We were discussing how various charities work with these horses with the aim to eventually put them back out into private ownership, where they can enjoy a well-earned and gentle retirement.

Anyway, we were filming in a stable yard and then going out for a good old ride with these retired racehorses. As we rode the horses calmly up a lane, there was an electric fence on our right-hand side and a hedgerow on the left. At the time, a farmer was sitting in his tractor on his lunch break, whilst working on the opposite side of the hedge, totally out of sight. He was completely unaware we were there and, unfortunately, just as we got level with him, he started up the loud engine of his tractor and powerful hedge cutter.

My horse was instantly startled. She skipped to the right, burned her leg on the electric fence, which scared her, causing her to rear up and hit the electric fence again, this time with her back legs. This sudden panic caught me by total surprise and, through no fault of anybody's, I was thrown off.

Worst of all, my horse then fell backwards and landed on me.

I immediately felt my back was hurt but I quickly stood up and the adrenaline diffused some of the pain. I told my colleagues I was all right to continue and film the link for the end of the show.

'So, thanks for watching *Countryfile* . . . And hopefully we will see you next week . . .'

I got back home to the Chilterns and said to Nicola who, as you know, is a trained physio, 'Nicola, I've had a bit of an accident . . .'

'OK, what's gone on?' she said.

'A horse fell on me.'

From the tone of her reaction, I could tell she was obviously pretty concerned.

'Can you move your toes OK?'

'Well, funny you say that, my feet feel a bit weird . . .'

She wasn't impressed.

We drove straight to hospital but when we arrived, Nicola wouldn't let me get out of the car so we parked up by the ambulances, they took a few minutes examining me then said they needed to lift me out and carry me through to a ward for some X-rays.

It turned out that I'd fractured my back.

Nicola had guessed this might be the case, which was why she was so adamant that I didn't twist and climb out of the car. While I was in the car on the way to the hospital, the seat had supported my back and kept it in one position. Had I climbed out, I could've caused even more damage.

I should qualify that and say that I'd not fully broken my back, but I'd fractured it enough to require a back support for weeks and weeks and, boy, it was painful! I'd snapped the wings on the vertebrae so the best thing to do . . . was just do nothing. The prescribed treatment was to basically rest a lot and essentially do nothing until the bones had fused. It wasn't a clean break so the recovery period was around four months. The problem was, you may have guessed that I am not one for doing nothing, so that was a very frustrating time for me. It was also very painful, even with medication designed to help with all the aches and pains. I had to wear a back support for a few months as well and, to this day, I still have a lot of trouble with it. I don't think my back has ever been as strong as it was before the accident.

The whole experience knocked my confidence with horse riding, if I am being honest with you. That said, it could have been worse and I lived to fight another day!

These two painful anecdotes are really exceptions to the rule. I find horses incredible animals really – I absolutely do – and I've had almost entirely fabulous experiences with them. They are so regal. The sheer size of them is breathtaking, but there's also a serenity and aura around horses that I find very appealing. They are such big animals but usually have

143

the temperament of a mouse; sometimes the tiniest little thing will panic them.

You don't want to order these amazing creatures about, that just isn't going to work. They are gentle souls, so I treat them as such. I almost feel like you have to be a centaur, the mythical creature who was half-man, half-horse! By that I mean you need to become 'one' with your horse, not in any hippy way, but in terms of the understanding between you both – the horse is part of you and you are part of the horse. The communication that goes on between you and the horse is just so rewarding, so energizing and so natural. I love riding horses, it is such a beautiful experience, something I never tire of.

As well as the elegant horses, we have some much smaller equine friends living with us on the farm – Mediterranean miniature donkeys. These were originally bred in Sardinia and Sicily, as shepherds' helpers and companions. Our donkeys' ancestors had a tough life back in the day. Turning grinding wheels blindfolded, walking in endless circles to crush grain, or being used to take supplies up the steep mountains for shepherds.

The concept of having them live with us came from a *Countryfile* Christmas Special where we were doing a kind of Nativity feature. On the day of filming the stable scene, a lady brought one of these donkeys along and I was instantly hooked.

*Oh, my word, these are absolutely incredible!*

I literally fell in love with them, and rang my mum straight away. She made some phone calls, went and sussed them out and we quickly ended up with five of them!

We have Winifred, Luna (born at night, hence the name), Pavlova, Augustine and Sophia – initially, the idea was that we would breed them, sell the males and keep the females, but we have only ever had female foals, so the little herd just keeps on growing! Sophia had already given birth to Augustine when she arrived and later had another foal, which was Luna. Winifred came to the farm with Sophia and Augustine and had a foal herself that we called Pavlova. There're more exciting times ahead for our herd as we'll be pairing them with a red-coloured jack.

The term 'miniature' is apt as they are only 32 inches to their withers (base of the neck above the shoulder). For Mum, this is a perfect grooming height as they love nothing more than leaning into your body as you brush their winter coats to reveal the most beautiful greys with chocolate highlights, brown, black and slate grey. You can also get spotted, two-tone and creamier colours that are definitely on Mum's radar, but these variants are yet to grace our donkey paddock!

They all have a much more relaxed existence in our Durham valley than their hard-working ancestors in the Mediterranean. These days, the only help they offer us is as companions and as a therapeutic tool and barometer of how you're feeling. You see, these miniature donkeys are remarkably affectionate and have the most beautiful aura. When you are around them, you always feel calm (apart from when they send out their booming morning wake-up calls!). They come straight up to you and it feels almost spiritual; they've got an incredible energy about them. Ironically, for all of their wonderfully serene aura, they're tough little things, they are: they will stand up to a lion!

Mum is obsessed with them – they are magical. They are more of a farming ornament, just quirky as pie and so beautiful! That's a bit harsh actually – because those donkeys are the most incredible way to centre yourself; they are just this source of stripping back the layers of modern life and calming your spirit. When you are in their presence, nothing matters. If you are flapping about and being noisy, they won't come over to you and that instantly reminds you to put your feelings to one side. It is a really good exercise to walk into that paddock and see what reaction you get. Horses are the same; if you go out for a ride and you're stressed and tense, they pick up on that straight away, so you just have to acknowledge how you are feeling, step back from the tension, and just tune into the animal.

We have four donkey stables that we muck out regularly. They get a new bed every day (or sometimes every other day, depending on how busy we are), but we aim to clear it out as regularly as possible. As well as their paddocks, they also have a yard which they run around in and they like to mess that up as well, so you've got to be regularly sweeping your yards and clearing all that. You sweep out all the muck, jetwash it all down, then put some fresh straw back. We need to look after their feet, so clean bedding is vital – donkeys don't wear metal shoes like horses, so we have to get a farrier in every six weeks to file down their feet.

I love mucking out the donkeys because I don't mind the smell of donkey muck at all (even though it lingers!), and I really like the idea of preparing this lovely, fresh bed for them, giving them new straw every day. They've got large rubber mats in there as well, which not only stop them from slipping but also help to keep the stable floor nice and warm.

These miniature donkeys have acquired a taste for our ancient meadow hay. They were used to other much more plain feed because they are bred to live on mountains where there is no hay; when we first started feeding them our delicious hay, you could literally see them thinking, *Hang on a minute, this tastes amazing, this is the good stuff!* That hay is so nutritious. It's really funny – I think if we tried to go back to a more conventional diet for them now, we'd have a donkey mutiny on our hands!

Mum seems obsessed with small animals now, which is great in terms of the physical demands of the farm moving forward. At the end of the donkey stables we also have the pygmy goats, Brookie and Bourbon. We moved them in there to make it easier for Mum to feed up. Then we went and got a fantastic-looking billy goat, all covered in wispy, long hair, who Mum said looked like Gandalf from *Lord of the Rings*. The pygmy goats are great neighbours for the miniature donkeys; they live really well together. The goats don't get mucked out as regularly as the donkeys because they actually prefer their own solid bed. It's certainly not dirty, by any means, and that is helped by the fact their poos are just little pellets (they look a little bit like chocolate raisins, although I don't recommend trying to see if they taste like that!). The pygmy goats are so funny and characterful.

When I was younger, we had Saanen and Anglo Nubian goats, which are milkers – we would milk these goats before we went to school. My sister suffered from eczema and after my mum read claims that goat's milk helps with that condition, we started having that on our cereal. She was just trying to find a way to help my sister. Then Mum started making cottage cheese from goat's milk and stuff like that – she loved the goats so much. The pygmy goats are just another way for her to continue having the animals she loves but in a way that is manageable.

When grandkids started to become a possibility in the family, Mum took the opportunity to get the 'perfect pony' for future kids. He was a Shetland called Beano and we adored him. I've always had a soft spot for Shetlands because, like the majority of rural children, I learned to ride on one (with Shandy).

Shetlands are a rock-hard breed and we loved having them grace our farm. They can cope with shortages of natural food and are mega-strong for their size; in fact, a Shetland can pull twice its weight, whereas a massive draught horse can only haul half its weight.

Beano was a beautiful Shetland but he came with a caveat – he arrived with his pal Dandy who, to be honest, was as wrong as Beano was right! Beano was a blue roan, with perfect quarters, a beautiful thick black mane and a tail long enough to offer extra protection from the westerly wind. On the other hand, Dandy was a milky cream, pigeon-toed stallion with a twitch and cross-eyes. He may not have won any 'best of breed' competitions, but he was full of character and fitted in on the farm like a hand in a glove. He lived happily until he was sixteen, while Beano lasted well into his thirties!

Beano was an amazing character, who seemed to love the cold more than the sunshine. Whenever we had a big snowstorm, he used to stand out in the drifts, facing the wind. It could be absolutely freezing and up to your waist in drifts and yet there he was, facing the storm. He wouldn't even go into his wonky little field shelter. Sometimes we would actually have to dig our way through the snow to get to him and make sure he was OK. This always puzzled me and I couldn't work out what was going on . . .

'What are you doing, Beano?'

Then, one year, I did a short film about reindeer and the expert we spoke to explained that when it was really bad weather, you would see the reindeer turn into the wind because that pushed their coat down against their body and insulated them from the extremes, as well as making the most of their body profile being at its smallest in that direction. I immediately thought, *That's what Beano does!* He was a rock-hard little nutter. One of many absolutely wonderful characters that we have been lucky enough to have on the farm.

# 6

# Autumn

I think that the change from summer to autumn is perhaps the most dramatic of all the seasonal shifts. There is a definite, quite sudden change in the weather, something incredibly strong that instigates the shutdown of trees and everything else . . . When you are on the farm and in among it when that switch happens, it is very evident. Sometimes it takes place within a couple of days, you see this chain reaction and watch this winding down; you see how quickly the leaves turn and everything retracts.

I often think autumn is almost like nature holding its breath – like before you are just about to submerge for a big, long underwater swim; that's what autumn feels like to me, this big breath in, then everything is holding on through the winter before they can breathe out again in spring.

I absolutely love the colours of autumn, all those rich, rusty tones. Breathtaking. Everything seems to suddenly blend and merge . . . those colours: the browns, the oranges, the reds, the green tones that hang on through it as well – I find that very relaxing and calming. You could almost think of the landscape wearing a different wardrobe through the seasons, and certainly autumn would be khaki throughout these months. I also like that you do need to wrap up but not so much that you feel suffocated, you just feel cosy and warm – I like the temperatures of autumn.

Autumn is also a big time of celebration in our family – we love Halloween and Bonfire Night, although obviously the downside of the latter is you have to be very mindful of frightening animals, so we don't use any fireworks. We have a lot of family get-togethers around this time as well, and it starts to feel like the run-up to Christmas. Of course, autumn is also when I start to gear up for my Rickshaw Challenge – which I will come to shortly!

One of the key jobs on the farm every autumn is tending to our hedgerows. Farmers were using hedgerows many centuries ago and the history books tell us that armies in the first century BC used huge hedgerows to create massive obstacles for their enemies in battle. Shakespeare even mentions 'a thick pleached alley' in *Much Ado About Nothing*, so my family farm is in fine company! Hedgerows were also popular in gardens up until the late eighteenth century, essentially as 'living fences'. Believe it or not, some hedgerows in the UK are believed to be over eight hundred years old!

However, when my parents bought the farm, there weren't any hedgerows at all, due to the history of the place, having been part of the Coal Board estate. That was one of the first ideas they had to help rejuvenate and change how the farm worked. They started to plant all the hedgerows that we have bordering the various fields and boundaries. What you see here now is the result of many years of effort on their part to rectify that missing piece of their jigsaw: all these magnificent mature hedgerows with hawthorn, blackthorn, hazel, rowan, dog rose and holly, a perfect wildlife city, complete with all amenities ready for species to move in.

'Laying' a hedgerow requires very specific, trad-itional expertise. The little saplings and whips are planted and then, when they get to a certain height and stem width, spliced, then bent sideways – and this is where the real skill comes in – they are then interwoven into a lattice of small branches. You want plenty of height so that enough species can thrive in there. Typically, you might wait till the hedgerow is around three to five metres tall. By then, you will also have a good old width going on, too. At that point, you 'pleach' it. Pleaching (also known by some as 'plashing') is when you cut the branch but not all the way through, you leave enough on there uncut so that the sap can continue to run through (this will keep the plant alive and strong), and then bend the branch into the woven lattice. Over time, the new shoots grow up towards the light, so you wait till you think the size is correct once again, you pleach again, weave it in again, then on you go. Sometimes cer-tain branches might fuse together naturally and, over time, if you have judged your pleaching right, the hedge will get thicker and stronger and increasingly complex, like a natural, woven basket. Our hedges are kept at a minimum of two metres by two metres and those that are cut are on a rotation, meaning they aren't cut every year. So laying a network of hedges right across the farm is a constant and very skilled task, but it's so rewarding to see all these magnificent mature hedgerows and to know how much good they are doing for the farm's ecosystem.

Over time, these hedgerows take on a life of their own. They evolve under their own steam and various species just spontaneously start to live there. You survey the hedge and it can be breathtaking how many species are living there, yet they haven't been put there by a human hand, they just moved in of their own accord. Believe it or not, the variety, amount and type of species present in there can even help you age a hedge really quite accurately.

Hedgerows are not just a magnificent sight, they are also an absolute lifeline for so many species. What my mum and dad have very cleverly done is use the new hedgerows to create these vast corridors, safe havens if you like, in which the small animals, insects and all sorts of little creatures can move around the farm safely and away from predators. They can run from one side of the farm to the other completely undercover.

You might wonder how many creatures live in a hedgerow . . . you'd be amazed. According to John Craven's *Countryfile Handbook*, one single hawthorn can support around 149 species, making it an incredible miniature ecosystem for its size. Basically, you look after the little guys, the insects, and bring them in, and everything else will follow, such that you end up with this incredible support system that can run undercover and gets to where it needs to go.

My favourite species in our hedges are the robust blackthorn and hawthorn. Both are hermaphrodite, which means both male and female parts are in each flower. Early-flowering blackthorn provides a valuable source of nectar and pollen for bees in spring. One type of berry in abundance in our hedgerows are sloes, the produce of the blackthorn, black fruits measuring about a centimetre across. A blackthorn will grow up to seven metres tall, if left alone, and could well stick around for a hundred years, judging by the height of some of the species down in the woods, which are definitely approaching a century old! I also love the shape of the crisp white hawthorn flower with its five petals and gentle pinky parts.

When pollinated by the abundance of insects that make use of our hedgerows, it's these flowers that turn into the deep red fruit known as 'haws' – hence the name. Its leaves give food to the caterpillars of loads of different moths and butterflies, including the magpie and swallow-tailed moths and the black and brown hairstreak butterflies. Seeing birds flying with sheep fleece in their beaks to line their nests and feasting on the caterpillars and everything else living off the leaves and taking the sloes in autumn or the seed husks, all reminds me exactly how a hedge amazingly sustains so much life as it matures.

Over the years, I've made many a walking stick from blackthorn and hazel. In days gone by, blackthorn was used for tool handles, from axes to brooms ... and I don't just mean yard brooms, because blackthorn was also associated with witches as the chosen material for their wands and staffs. On a magical theme, it's also been used for all sorts of remedies throughout history. Potions have been made from the flowers, the bark and the sloes for rheumatism and as a means of cleansing the blood, among other uses. Even their colouring is useful: with hedges being deciduous, they take on different characteristics through the year and it's their green haze that tells us that the farm is about to burst back into life after a tough winter.

Sadly, despite their multitude of uses, planting new hedgerows hasn't been normal practice for some years across much of the UK, not least because establishing them is not an easy task, nor is it a quick one. As a consequence, these old traditional skills are at risk of being lost. A lot of the hedgerows on our island have been taken out due to modern farm machinery being so big; you can't turn tractors around so easily if the fields are divided up by hedgerows. Of course, on our farm we aren't arable and therefore don't grow crops in this way, so my parents have spent years planting hedgerows that are now very mature, just the most wonderful sight. (Thankfully, there are schemes to help put back as many hedgerows as possible, working with farmers to come up with the best solutions going forward.)

Funnily enough, one person I often think of when I am around hedgerows is Prince Charles! Back in 2013, he was the guest editor of *Countryfile* and we were looking into the heritage skills and crafts that he and his team use on the Duchy of Cornwall Estate. It's a topic that he is really incredibly passionate about.

It was a brilliant morning: I remember it well. We were doing a few little pieces to camera before Prince Charles was due to turn up, just so that we were ready to go straight into the filming when he arrived, because we didn't want to waste any of his time. As I was chatting away to camera, we noticed these two blokes wandering up the field; they were in the back of the shot the whole time, just strolling along, quietly chatting. We moved the camera slightly so that we could get the filming done without these two blokes in shot . . . but they just kept walking closer and closer . . . until finally the penny dropped . . . it WAS Prince Charles! No entourage, no big fuss, he just walked over, introduced himself and shook my hand.

I will never forget that handshake, because I can tell you that he has a farmer's hand, that square palm, that real good, firm handshake and the thickness of his reassuring grip that can only come from years of actually working on farms. That's not a handshake that you can buy into or fake – it's earned. Definitely a farmer's handshake.

We talked about wildlife and then about hedges at length, and it was plain to see he has a real passion for the countryside and farming. That was a real eye-opener for me. That notion of a person's background on a farm is real and you can just sense it straight away. As we chatted more, you could tell from what he was saying that he obviously works on his estate himself. He just wouldn't know as much intricate detail as he does if he simply paid someone else to do everything. Despite his unique upbringing and family circumstances, he is obviously a very practical man.

We worked on some hedge-laying together and he knew exactly what he was doing. I remember vividly that he was wearing this old coat that was all patched up; it was totally fascinating, all higgledy-piggledy, ripped, resewn and patched up with all different scraps of wax jackets and other coats – it was mesmerizing to look at.

Another area that Prince Charles was passionate about was heritage breeds, so we talked at length about that topic. Once again, he really knew his stuff. He has a number of heritage county breeds on his estate that are much less commonplace nowadays. Again, he knew about each breed's history, their subtle differences, the various approaches to caring for them; it just felt like two farmers having a chat. And just like any other farmer I might meet and talk to, I was admiring his Hebridean flock and said, 'Oh, I'd love to buy some!'

Well, come on, if you were in my wellies, you'd say the same thing, wouldn't you?

Much to my complete amazement, Prince Charles said, 'OK, great, let's work something out!' We chatted, did a deal and then the Prince put me in touch with his head shepherd, who was in charge of his flock. He was fantastic, really helpful and accommodating, and before long we ended up with sheep from the Duchy estate, so now we have what you could call a right royal flock!

I have been taught to always take people as you find them. With someone as famous and high profile as Prince Charles, we have all grown up with so many stories, opinions and ideas about what he is like, but when I meet anyone, be it on the farm or while I am filming, I will always just take them as I find them. When you present TV programmes, you always get given research about a guest that (out of necessity) summarizes them in easily digestible chunks, but often you will find they are completely different in person to your preconception.

When we had finished filming, we chatted some more and then it was time for Prince Charles to leave. He walked up to the farmyard and climbed into a fairly beaten-up old car, nothing fancy, just a farmer's workhorse of a vehicle . . . and off he went. I've heard it said that the Queen likes nothing more than putting on her wax jacket and jumping into a Land Rover to go out on the farm with her dogs. It is obvious that Charles clearly loves being out in nature, with animals, around farming and the countryside, and although in every other aspect our lives are totally different in every conceivable way, I can absolutely relate to that particular compulsion. I found Prince Charles to be a friendly, passionate and fascinating farmer with a deep knowledge of the countryside and an eagerness to talk to like-minded people.

Another of our autumn jobs on the farm is 'Tupping Time', which is when you mate the male sheep (tup) to the female (ewe). An experienced tup might mate with up to fifty ewes, so they are very busy sheep – therefore you need a system in place to keep track of what has been going on, between whom and when! Ewes will typically be around two or three years of age before they start to be used for breeding; the tups can be as young as eighteen months or so.

When the time comes for the tups to have their time with the ladies, you put a raddle harness on them that is belted round their back and middle, and that carries a big wax crayon that sits in this harness around their chest. You choose your tup based on which one you think has the best physical attributes and he gets the lucky ticket, so to speak. Then, when he jumps up on to the back of the female to do his duty (to 'serve her'), this wax crayon rubs a specific colour on her back so that you know which tup did his duty with which ewe. You change the colour of the raddle every two weeks or so, in order to know with greater precision when certain ewes were served and therefore when they will be due to lamb. This is important because you need to know when ewes may need to be brought inside or watched more carefully as the birth approaches.

The raddle's 'crayon' is quite a modern system really, but back in the day farmers used to literally slop different-coloured paint on – in some of the more harsh environments, you still see that because it tends to be more durable than the crayon substitute.

You need to be precise because generally ewes only come into season once a year. There are certain breeds like Hampshires that are an exception to this and you can lamb them at Christmas or spring-time, but in both cases the window of opportunity is relatively brief; you leave your tup in with the ewes for at least six weeks, which allows the ewes to have two cycles. As I mentioned earlier, if you put your tups in on Bonfire Night, then the gestation period means that you get 1 April lambs. It's as precise as that – around 145 days, or four and a half months. Remember that old farming saying? 'In with a bang and out like fools!'

This all sounds very precise and scientific but I have to admit that tupping doesn't always go exactly to plan. Although farms can be very dangerous places, and you do sadly hear of some pretty nasty accidents, we work very hard to make ours safe and the fact we only manage a hundred acres of low-intensity farm, using very few machines, helps us stay out of danger. I rolled a tractor once, which was all very dramatic: I hadn't noticed a drop to one side of the tractor so when I swung around, it flipped over. I was fine though. I think the worst injury I've sustained, luckily, was a dislocated thumb from sorting out the tups for tupping! That was just funny, to be honest, painful but funny. I was catching a tup that was called Two Great White Sharks (we always name our tups). She said we needed to come up with a name for this particular tup, but we got a cross-wire when I told her this joke:

'Two great white sharks were cruising round a swimming pool one weekend.

'One turns to the other and says, "Don't you think it's quiet for a Saturday?"'

(If, like my daughter, you don't get this joke . . . there's no one in the water because of the sharks.)

My mum misheard me and thought I was offering a name up for this new tup! Anyway, 'Two Great White Sharks' stuck!

So, I was wrestling with this tup called Two Great White Sharks, trying to lift up its chin so that it didn't run forwards. For one reason or another, I didn't quite get my hand in the right position and he butted my thumb and dislocated it. It's never been right since, especially when it's cold. However, Mum's nasty accident aside, I am well aware that a dislocated thumb is a pretty small injury from a lifetime of farming, so no complaints!

Back when I was a teenager, I used to be quite useful at rugby, but any skills I had on the sports field were entirely trained into me by farm work. I tell you what, if you want to get good and strong at tackling a large, speeding rugby player, there's no better way to get ready for that than by grabbing hold of a massive great tup who doesn't want to be caught.

Now, on the farm we have a passageway between two fields we call the 'gath': it's an old-fashioned term to describe a connecting bit of land from one field to another. So way back when I was about thirteen years old, we had got all these sheep in the gath and I was desperate to dive in and grab this one particular tup, so that we could change the crayon on his raddle.

'Don't you worry, Mum, I've got this all under control . . .'

I went in there and grabbed this massive tup, got hold of him and there was no way I was letting go, literally *no way*. Anyway, in the mêlée, the gate to the top meadow suddenly burst open because it was only fastened with a piece of string that I hadn't tied properly. Of course, as soon as the sheep saw the open gate, the entire flock turned to run out . . . including the tup I had a hold of . . . but there was still NO WAY that I was letting go of this great big sheep.

The problem was, he really, *really* wanted to run with the flock, so he was dragging me along the rubbly gath and I was digging my heels in to try and stop him. I could feel the ground was cutting up underneath me; I half fell under him, then I somehow regained my balance and was back behind him, pulling, dragging, doing anything I could to win this particular battle.

Eventually, this tup gave in; he stopped running and stood still.

TRIUMPH! YES!

'There you go, Mum, what did I tell you! All under control, eh?'

Then I looked down.

In the carnage, I had ripped my shirt all the way down my back and the only evidence left that I'd been wearing tracksuit bottoms was the elastic round my ankles and around my waistband. I was standing there in a windswept field, completely covered in mud all over my bare, grazed legs, my shirt billowing in the breeze.

'Oh, yes, Matthew,' said my mum, 'I can see . . . totally under control.'

*

We don't plough our land or anything on the farm, but typically autumn is the time when farmers are out in the fields for incredibly long hours getting their land turned over. Ploughing is simply that, the process of turning over the soil so that you get rid of the weeds or the roots of the last crop, literally in the same way that you would do in a vegetable patch – you dig down, you flip it over and that stops the light getting in, which prevents any photosynthesis. It also ploughs in any stubble that you may have left over as a crop, such as wheat or barley.

Although we don't grow any crops, I still love a bit of ploughing! One time on *Countryfile*, I was privileged to be able to try ploughing a square on a Ferguson TE20 (the name is short for 'Tractor England 20 Horsepower'). Now, in case you haven't heard of that machine, let me explain: it is a little grey tractor that was an incredibly pioneering vehicle following its initial release in 1946. Over the ten or so years that it was manufactured, the 'Little Grey Fergie', as it became known, proved to be a farmer's favourite – nimble, light, small and extremely versatile. It became an icon of the farming world and, to this day, collectors cherish them. Remarkably, plenty are still in active service, seventy or so years later. This particular tractor is so famous that there was even an album made by

Australian folk musician Peter Pentland, called *Me Beaut Little Fergie Tractor*.

Part of the appeal of the Little Fergie was the system that the tractor's designer, Harry Ferguson, added: a seminal three-point hitch (or linkage) system which pretty soon became widely adopted in farming. This allowed a farmer to quickly and easily attach all sorts of implements such as ploughs to the tractor. The three points resemble a triangle, similar to the letter 'A', and, crucially, they keep the implement in a fixed position, with the two hydraulic arms at the bottom lifting it up and down. This made this system much more controlled for the farmer, compared to older systems. Ferguson himself had actually patented his design as far back as 1926, but it was the Little Fergie that popularized his specific system worldwide. It was so versatile that you could use something like sixty or more implements on the tractor with it. The system was so well designed that it is still the industry standard to this day.

Alongside Russian gymnast Valeri Liukin – the first person to do a triple back somersault on floor – these tractors were what I had posters of on my bedroom wall: they were so admired, so popular, I just loved them. So you can imagine, when *Countryfile* decided to do a feature on this tractor as a celebration of its seventieth anniversary, I was very excited. As part of the transition from ploughing with a horse to always using a tractor, the manufacturers liked to show that the machines could plough a small square, and over time this has become a competitive sport! There are very specific techniques that I was shown for ploughing this square and on the day of filming I was just obsessed with doing a really neat job. I always say I will buy a TE20 one day. The noise, the smell, the sound of these wonderful little tractors are all just so lovely to me.

The first autumn after my mum had her accident, we planted a new orchard in the old hill garden, something that had always been my dad's dream. That area has excellent hedgerows around it which provide good shelter from the wind, plus it is south facing. That said, a thousand feet above sea level can be a challenging site to grow apples on. There is a shorter growing season, the winds can be incredibly high, the soil quality will sometimes be less than perfect . . . but we wanted to have a go anyway!

According to some sources, apple trees originated in the high plateaus of central Asia and, in the modern day, there are not many wild apple forests left, such as those found in the Tian Shan mountain range of southern Kazakhstan. Apples are grown throughout the world in a staggering variety of locations including in the Himalayas and on the Tibetan plateau. So, there is obviously proof that apples can thrive at higher altitudes, and, by comparison, at a thousand feet above sea level, our farm is relatively 'lowly'. That said, I think it is fair to point out that the most productive orchards, certainly in the UK, are those cider-growing areas that are warmer than where we are.

One element of planting an orchard that you may not have heard of is 'grafting'. I don't mean the hard work, that's a given on any farm! Grafting with regards to trees is a very specific process which aims to evolve the tree species by blending two different varieties together. It is a really remarkable concept that very clever botanists have come up with over the years.

Each tree's 'root stock' (essentially a developed root system) holds all the information about how that tree is going to grow. The actual stem (often called the 'scion wood') holds the information about the variety of fruit that you will get. What botanists did many, many years ago was come up with the idea of grafting, which allows you to connect the two parts together, so you can have whatever variety of fruit you want, but grown in a way that you want it to grow.

The trees we bought needed to be more mature for us to put them in without them being shocked, so they had already been grafted. You take a short piece of the scion wood, often a small branch or twig, and then cut it in a very specific way – to use the technical terms, you cut 'matching clean elliptical slices' – the idea being that when you join the two parts together, generous sections of the exposed wood are touching each other. This creates a really strong structural graft that you know won't fail. It's mind blowing. I actually went to the National Orchard and I watched all their grafters – it's so skilful. Nicola loves grafting; it can be really relaxing and deeply rewarding when it works well. Ideally, you need to do this work when the tree is dormant, so that it is not desperately trying to sprout and grow . . . if it's in that dormant stage, then it has time to settle before it wakes up and cracks on in the spring.

This method can give you great flexibility about what you grow. What we ended up doing for my mum and dad's orchard gives them all the varieties that they like, but in a way that is easy for them to harvest. If you go to these big orchard farms, all the trees are grown for harvesting using specialist machinery. That's not an option for my parents, but then neither is reaching down for hours on end to pick the fruit off the ground or climbing ladders to reach up high.

Instead, we picked a nice selection of varieties that will fruit at head height, but are also never going to be too tall that the wind will batter them when it comes down the valley – they will be squat enough to be able to cope with the harsh gusts.

We planted a good selection of species that included six apple varieties – Ribston Pippin, Cox's, Lady of the Lake, Beauty of Bath, Greensleeves and a very apt variety known as 'Baker's Delicious'! Our choice of varieties was also made by taking into consideration the landscape and environment of our particular farm, so they are on the hardier end of the species – with our apple ancestors in the Himalayas in mind. We also put a plum tree in there, too. I used a mini digger to scrape a level grass path running through the centre, so that it would be nice and easy to access these head-high fruit and pick them. I can see why my dad always wanted an orchard. There is something very special about eating your own apples.

It's not just the orchard that is cherished in terms of new trees on our farm. In certain areas of our acres, we have planted native tree species every twenty metres for birds to have lookout posts and other nesting opportunities. Oak, field maple and ash have been added to the range of trees that we already have on the farm.

Also, my dad is very sentimental about trees and always plants them in remembrance of family and friends when they pass on. In his words, it's 'nicer than a bunch of flowers and when you walk past that tree you think of that person'. I also get an enormous sense of legacy as you watch that tree react to the seasons and observe the wildlife making a home there, feeling that person's spirit live on: from Uncle Tony, Aunty Ivy, Uncle Charlie and Aunty Annie, along with the new pink-blossoming cherry that Mum has just planted in the front field for my wonderful Grandpa, who got to the age of ninety-eight. He loved pink ties and pink V-neck sweaters, so the blossom is just perfect and I can't wait to see his favourite vibrant colour sing out in the valley.

In 2006, after almost eight years on *Blue Peter*, presenting over seven hundred programmes and making more than three hundred films, I left that telly institution. Whenever I presented *Blue Peter*, I wasn't talking to seven-year-olds in my mind, I was just telling a story and I didn't think about how old the viewers were – besides, back then we had quite a cult audience with plenty of students and members of the older generation, people who watched afternoon quiz shows, all sorts. So it felt like quite a broad age range, more of a family show than kids' telly. I would like to think it was a golden age of *Blue Peter*: our viewing figures were as brilliant as ever and the four of us – Simon Thomas, Konnie Huq, Liz Barker and myself – stuck together. That was my dream team. We all had our little quirks, and we all knew what each other did well, so that we'd automatically know who was going to do which story. The laughs that we had were off the scale – really wonderful times! I view those times as so precious; I'll be forever grateful.

I am very proud to have won two consecutive BAFTAs for 'Best Children's Presenter', as well as a Royal Television Society Award. In the immediate aftermath, I did quite a range of programmes. I did a couple of series of *City Hospital* in the morning with Nadia Sawalha, which was a live show based in a hospital where we were reporting back on people's operations, being in theatres and A & E and what have you; I absolutely loved that. I also did a new show called *Animal Rescue*, live from Battersea Dogs & Cats Home with Selina Scott, which was a very comfortable fit for me, given my love of dogs.

It was around this period that I played Caractacus Potts in a production of *Chitty Chitty Bang Bang* at the Sunderland Empire. I had done a story while on *Blue Peter* about that famous musical when it was on at the London Palladium, where I joined the cast of dancers and went behind the scenes; it was brilliant. At the time, the producer, Michael Rose, said to me, 'When you are done with *Blue Peter*, let me know because I'd like to put you in the show.'

Well, fast-forward to 2008 and, sure enough, I'd left *Blue Peter* and Michael was good for his word! This time it was a little more local to the farm, so it was great fun; the Empire was also somewhere that I'd been to many times, so I liked that. While I was working at the Empire, myself, Nicola, Dad and a pal of his turned our byre into a bedsit at the side of the house, lined the walls and reroofed it – that place was so cosy. I have incredibly fond memories of that time – our first-born Luke was very little, I was working locally so I got to see him loads, I was living the dream.

Then, one day in 2009, I was contacted by Jay Hunt, who was the Controller of BBC One at the time. She had seen me doing various bits and pieces on the farm on *Blue Peter* and knew of my rural background.

She explained that the plan was to shift *Countryfile* to an evening slot, and asked if I would be interested in coming on board to present.

Now, at the time, this was actually quite a controversial move. Prior to that, *Countryfile* had always been on a Sunday morning, around 11 a.m., and was very well established in that slot, not least with a lot of farmers who would come in from feeding around that time of the morning and watch for the weather forecast. So to shift what was regarded as an iconic programme to a prime-time evening slot was a brave move.

Regardless of the scheduling, I was so excited to be asked to be on *Countryfile*. I had watched that show since I was a kid, and I had grown up with some of its presenters. Most obviously, like anyone my age, I watched *John Craven's Newsround* religiously, so I felt like he had been there all my life. When John moved to *Countryfile*, I went with him there as a fan, too.

The BBC wanted to try and turn *Countryfile* into more of a family/lifestyle show and asked me if I would bring my experience and expertise of children's television along with me, as well as – hopefully – a younger audience.

At the time, I didn't really know what direction I was going to go in or where I wanted to be. However, to be offered *Countryfile* was a huge opportunity so I grabbed it with both hands. On the show were myself, Julia Bradbury, John Craven and Adam Henson, and the format was very much that Julia and I would go off on an adventure to whatever county we were featuring, John would be doing the investigations and Adam would be based on his own farm. This worked really well and the newly formatted and scheduled show quickly became very popular.

I didn't change my presenting style at all for *Countryfile*. People seemed to be receptive to my life on the farm and the angles that I was coming at each story from. For me, it was all about storytelling again, just chatting to people and hearing what they were up to. When people realized that I knew what they were talking about and that I was on the same wavelength, they were more open to me straight away. So many guests said they expected us to turn up with all these vans and loads of crew: catering, make-up trucks and all of that, but usually it was literally three of us in a field. From the second we turned up, I would do my hellos and then say, 'Shall we just go and have a chat?'

I am proud to say that I was very heavily involved in those early days of reworking and reshaping that show into what became a massive TV hit. Despite the controversy, a lot of people loved the new show and time slot immediately, and ratings went through the roof – peaking at a record of over nine million (with regular figures of eight million).

To give *Countryfile* its full credit, the show became something of a TV juggernaut, because prior to that move, there wasn't any rural programming at all in that prime-time slot. Then, suddenly, we were getting millions of viewers so all the other channels woke up to this and started to commission rural shows. That was a pretty big sea change in UK TV programming.

I learned a lot from John Craven – obviously I

had followed him from when I was a kid and now, coincidentally, my own career was kind of mimicking his, in that I had done children's TV and now I'd migrated across into this rural programme. To this day, I love to catch up with John and hear his advice. He has been a real sounding board for me, and I have thoroughly enjoyed – and continue to enjoy – his company. John will always be a big part of the *Countryfile* family.

I've also learned so much from my actual job on *Countryfile* itself – because I go out every week and meet the most fascinating people, whether that's folk who are innovating and are on the cutting edge of modern farming or maybe people who have amazing traditional skills. For each series of that show, I get to hear hundreds of new ideas and old wisdoms – all sorts. I love to listen and chat to these people and then take these ideas back to our farm to see if they can be of any benefit to us there.

I think the new format of *Countryfile* in that evening slot worked because it was a window into a world that most people weren't familiar with, yet the show made it feel accessible. It made it fun and attractive for a whole family to sit down together in front of the TV and learn about chickens or ploughing or cattle, or whatever. *Countryfile* on a Sunday evening somehow seemed to make this whole world of nature and farming a very mainstream idea. I would suggest this was a particularly revealing window into that world for those that live in the city and more built-up areas. For me, if people do not know about farming and wildlife, how can they enjoy it? How can they protect it? How can they play their part? *Countryfile* was able to bring the whole of the country into a world they'd never previously been engaged with. That is a very powerful legacy and something that the show and its whole team should be very proud of.

The year after I started on *Countryfile*, I had a call about going on *Strictly Come Dancing*. It seemed like a fun idea, plus it appealed to the gymnast in me, so I agreed and started the training. I was not entirely surprised when the first show came round and they played on the 'gymnastic farmer' angle – that's pretty unusual! They dressed me up in this country outfit, including some brown flares which weirdly enough sort of harped back to my days travelling around performing in Disco Inferno. I came out doing a handspring and a flying cartwheel and after that it was a blast. I really enjoyed my time on that show and was very proud to come second, behind only the actor Kara Tointon. Kara was brilliant; as I said on the telly the night she won, if I had been at home, I'd have voted for her, too!

For a while, I'd been helping out on *The One Show*, a five-times-a-week programme that had established itself as the leading prime-time magazine show in the UK. I was really happy with the way that *Countryfile* was going, so I must admit it was never really on my radar to get a job at *The One Show* permanently, but then I was approached about being a regular presenter. Obviously, I was interested, as this was such a big show, but as I was still doing *Countryfile*, I had no idea how, or even if, this could work. I was working on *Countryfile* two days a week, but the new Controller, Danny Cohen, said he would move the schedule around so that I could do Monday through Thursday on *The One Show*, then as long as I could get to wherever I was needed by Friday morning, I could end the week working on *Countryfile*.

Danny said, 'Try it for six months and see how you get on.'

Nine years later I was still doing that crazy schedule every week!

Practically, it took some doing, I have to be honest. Straight after *The One Show* finished on a Thursday evening, I would travel to that week's *Countryfile* location, and the agreement was that I had to get there for dawn the next day. It didn't matter where on earth that was, it could be the Outer Hebrides, whatever, I had to be there to start filming. That often meant travelling through the night, so on many occasions I would work two days for *Countryfile* in the space of twenty-four hours. We would also have voice-overs to be doing to bind the show together ready for the Sunday evening, so all of that had to be taken into account as well. Along with being back on the farm as much as I possibly could, these were busy times!

Across nearly a decade on *The One Show*, I met some wonderful people and interviewed countless incredible celebrities, and have too many stories to share all of them here. From a personal point of view, in terms of myself and Nicola, my favourite story from *The One Show* actually dates way back to when I was performing in those disco shows as a teenager. One of the best songs to perform on the stage back then was Billy Ocean's 'Love Really Hurts Without You'. I used to act out all the lyrics: whenever he sang 'baby', I'd cradle my arms; for 'love', I would shove my hand up my shirt and then put my palm against my chest and flick my hand out so it looked like my heart beating; for 'really hurts' I used to rub two hands up at my eyes to mimic crying and so on. Maybe my personal favourite was when he sang, 'it's breaking my heart': I used to lift my leg up and snap an imaginary piece of wood over my knee! When Nicola was in the audience, I used to always do these actions and then point at her, so that became 'our song'.

Unbelievably, by a total and massive coincidence, on our tenth wedding anniversary, Billy Ocean came on *The One Show*! I invited Nicola along on the night and Billy had his guitar with him, so I asked him if he would play the song and he did, live on air! We headed backstage after the filming had finished and Billy was serenading us as we went down to the dressing room; it was incredible. He even signed my small, travelling guitar – unfortunately, I left this guitar in my dressing room over the summer and somehow it got broken. I was gutted but unbeknown to me, the *One Show* team replaced the guitar, sent it to Billy and he signed that new one for me. What a wonderful man.

The one abiding memory I will always have of my time on *The One Show* is a charity event that I am very proud of: the Rickshaw Challenge for Children in Need.

Initially, the idea came about as the result of a relatively simple remark, 'What can we do for Children in Need? Let's think of something special . . .' and the idea emerged of somehow visiting various towns around the country in some unusual way . . . then in no time at all this initial concept had morphed into travelling the full length of the UK! Once the notion of an endurance event down the length of the country was agreed, we started to think about *how* I might travel and that led to all sorts of crazy ideas, such as those old railway handcarts with huge see-saw levers that you often see in old black-and-white movies.

Then a chap from Children in Need by the name of Gareth Hydes said, 'What about a rickshaw, would you ever think about riding one of those?'

I instantly thought that was a great idea and pretty quickly we all got excited about the thought of me picking up 'cab fares', too, taking people on taxi rides. I remember saying at one point, 'I reckon we could raise quite a few thousand pounds by the time I get to London . . .'

To date, the Rickshaw Challenge has raised over £43 million.

The Great British public never cease to amaze me.

We got the first rickshaw rig from one of the Theatreland companies in central London, who use it to ferry tourists up and down the West End between restaurants and theatres. There were no modifications, it was just a rickshaw exactly like the ones you see being used on an evening in loads of city centres.

Usually these rickshaws are designed to ride about half a mile from a theatre to a restaurant or vice versa.

Here I was, planning on riding from Edinburgh to London.

That's 484 miles.

In just eight days.

I wouldn't have minded but it wasn't like I had ever really been a keen cyclist; I had a BMX when I was a kid but that was just me messing about around the village with my mates.

I tell you what, that very first rickshaw challenge was an almighty shock! I didn't get a chance to train properly. I cycled the thirty-five miles into work a few times but that wasn't very pleasant with all the traffic. Then I had a trip to Japan for the World Artistic Gymnastics Championships, so I came up with this masterplan to train for the challenge while I was out there. I arranged for a bike to be shipped out with me, and I was convinced that whenever I had downtime in between broadcasts, I would get in the saddle and ride miles and miles.

Do you know how many miles I covered in Japan?

Yup, zero.

I never even got on it. I worked really long hours, then when I got back to the hotel, I was usually too exhausted. The hotel room was so small I couldn't fit my bike into it, so it had to be stored somewhere else. And then I realized that the roads in Japan were so busy and complex that I wouldn't have the first clue where I was going. So, I actually never even sat on the bike while I was out there!

When you add to my lack of training the fact that it was only two years since I had broken my back after the horse fell on top of me while filming *Countryfile*, then, all things considered, I arrived at the starting point for my first Rickshaw Challenge in Edinburgh less than ideally prepared, to be honest!

On day one, after only thirty miles, I was already thinking, *Oh my gosh, what on earth have I done?*

Every mile was so draining. Whenever there was an incline it was like dragging a truck along, the rickshaw was so big and just unbelievably heavy.

And there were still 450-plus miles to go.

I was struggling to see how I could get to the end of that first day, never mind the entire route.

I was just thinking, *How on earth am I going to do this?*

The fifteen-geared bike itself was 13.5 stone (meaning in all, with me, it weighed about twenty-five stone) but on top of that we had fixed all this advertising boarding for Children in Need around it, so in terms of catching the wind, it was pretty disastrous. Early on, I remember coming into this valley not that far out of Edinburgh into a really strong headwind and the force was so strong that I literally just stopped. I couldn't pedal forward at all.

I stopped for a few seconds.

*How am I actually going to physically do this? I don't want to let anybody down but no one else can do this other than* me.

It was so overwhelming, to the point where I was in tears.

I had a choice: either finish now or finish in London.

That's when I did a reset.

It wasn't going to happen unless I changed my thinking.

Physically, it was going to be the hardest challenge I had ever faced.

I took a deep breath . . . and pushed on.

Once I had gone to that place, I was energized. I was meant to be turning up at various locations to do live broadcasts for *The One Show*, but more often than not, I just didn't get there in time. I realized that I needed to pace myself, so I apologized to people who were scheduled to meet me at the end of certain days and said, 'Look, I'm not going to be there at that time, I'm really sorry, but I WILL get there.'

I can honestly say that on that first Rickshaw Challenge, I went to a place that I've never been to before, not even when I was pushing and pushing for all my high-level gymnastics training and competitions.

I began most mornings at 4.30 a.m. and just started pedalling, almost without thinking. The sections of the route were broken down into daily chunks of between forty-one and seventy-eight miles, depending on the terrain and number of hills. Within a few days, I was having to switch to autopilot, because the physical challenge was proving so testing. I was adamant that no one was going to push or *even touch* the rickshaw; it had to all be me.

One of the very few negative aspects of my brilliant times doing gymnastics is that it has left me with less than perfect knees. I didn't realize at the time that the thousands and thousands of impacts during any performance or training regime were causing such damage to my knees – it's only later in life that you start to think, *Oh, gosh, I can't really bend down for longer than fifteen seconds!* That's not always ideal when you are working on a farm, but let me tell you, I found out exactly how bad my knees were when I did the Rickshaw Challenge! That first year, crikey, my knees were in bits. I had to learn to turn the cogs of the bike in a very smooth way to help my knees out but even then, to be honest, it was just a really painful experience. There were obviously thousands and thousands of repetitions each day – the longest day was something like ninety miles. Worse still, due to the set-up, I was having to do more pedalling than on a normal bike, so someone worked out that it was requiring about four times as many revolutions

– that's a lot of work for rickety knees! I was in agony a lot of the time.

At the end of each day, I had to have massages and ice baths to try to help my muscles recover. I was also having to try to eat nine thousand calories a day just to provide my exhausted body with enough energy. I tried some high-energy drinks but I didn't feel myself afterwards, so I kept the diet as natural as I could, eating lots of broccoli, spinach and plenty of fruit, chicken and eggs. While I was riding the rickshaw itself, I kept energy levels up by eating sausages, bananas, nuts and energy bars. In what little training I'd done, I'd had a few days where I drank water well but didn't eat enough and I soon found out – with stars in my eyes and a lot of feeling faint – that that was not the way to do it.

Back on the road, I started to notice people were really getting behind the challenge and supporting me brilliantly. You could see people thinking, *This lad's having a go here*. The donations started to pour in, the nationwide support was off the scale and I was getting people clapping me along the way, cheering, shouting . . . it was amazing.

The days went by quite fast after that (including riding through Lincoln, where I went on my first date with Nicola all those years before) and by the time I got to London, we had raised an unbelievable

£1.9 million! Incredible! I don't know how I did it, but I got there. The fascinating part in terms of the physicality of the challenge was that I had got myself into this zone, such a determined mindset, that when I finished, I was ready to turn round and ride back to Edinburgh! That first challenge was uncharted stuff for me and I am obviously very proud of what I achieved . . . but most of all it was the incredible support of the fundraiser by the public that just totally blew me away.

For the second year, I felt it needed to be about more than just someone off the telly raising money. I spoke to Nicola one night and said, 'Do you think it would be possible to highlight all those youngsters that had been through tough times and benefited from Children in Need and create a relay system where they join me on the ride?' She thought that was a great idea so I put it to *The One Show* and the Children in Need team and they went for it straight away!

We piloted the idea with a team of six youngsters to see how it might work and that's when Team Rickshaw was born and, crikey, that's become a massive part of my life now and I love every minute of it.

Over the years, we've assembled a remarkable, trusted team of people who create the safest environment for these youngsters to have the time of their lives. In a nutshell, I owe them so much for making my vision a reality. We cycle along together, with a camera set up in a vehicle driving some way ahead. However, you forget about that, because it just feels like it's us cycling along, having a chat. I always let them tell me their story, no preconceived ideas or plans, just chatting away and giving that young person the opportunity to talk about what they've been through. Due to the fact that I am not related to them and haven't been connected to their past, they start to tell me what they have experienced, sometimes in a way that they've never told anybody before. It's very special and I am privileged to be a part of that.

One unexpected benefit of these youngsters coming along with me on the ride is that they seem to blossom in terms of independence and confidence. These are young people who have been through very difficult, often excruciatingly challenging times, and so (totally understandably) their families are always keen to make sure they are OK, enjoying themselves, being looked after and maybe not trying to do something that they aren't capable of. In fact, I often have to reassure the families that their child is in safe hands and that we will slow down or even stop if we have to.

Every year, without fail, I watch these youngsters get on that rickshaw and just blossom and grow in the matter of a few miles. I just say to them, 'Right, off we go, first mile, here we go . . .' then if there is any sign they might be finding it tough, I say, 'Do you want to stop?'

And EVERY SINGLE TIME, they say, 'No, I'm not stopping, let's keep going!'

Another mile or two, then the chance to stop again . . .

'Let's keep going!'

By day two, they are banging out ten miles, easy!

Then something wonderful happens – their families see them in a way that they have never seen them before and they are totally gobsmacked and floored by what their wonderful children are achieving. It happens every year. For me that is the most incredible part of the whole thing – because at its heart, that is what Children in Need is all about: if you give a child an opportunity, give them a helping hand, show them the way, then you can step back and watch them fly. We aren't trying to break any records, there is no race with anyone else, so we just all dig in and get through the challenge together.

I am blessed to say the Rickshaw Challenge became a staple of Children in Need. As a consequence of this annual challenge, since 2011 I have been on the board of Children in Need – a great privilege. The board is a phenomenal group of the most . . . I don't like to use the word extraordinary too often . . . but they are extraordinary individuals, just the most incredible group of minds that come round a table from different worlds: TV, entertainment, marketing, business, accountancy; they are all there to get the most out of the donations that come in. I usually sit there thinking, *What the hell am I doing here, some bloke from the Durham Dales?*

Memorably, I used to sit beside the late great Sir Terry Wogan, who is actually the only person that I've ever been star-struck by. I went to interview him on *Blue Peter* one time, when I was doing a special about the Eurovision Song Contest, and when I saw him sitting behind his radio desk through the window, perfectly spotlit, reading his emails, I couldn't believe it: he took my breath away. I used to watch him on *Wogan* every night, so when I was on *The One Show* I loved that we had the same slot. Then, after we started with the rickshaw, I used to go and watch him from the sidelines doing his thing on *Children in Need*. I was fascinated because he would chat away to the audience before they were filming, then you would hear the credits rolling, then he would turn to the camera and just carry on chatting away in exactly the same manner! There was absolutely no difference in the tone of his voice or his approach. Impressive.

In our board meetings, Sir Terry would listen quietly and respectfully . . . and then say, 'What about the children? How does this benefit the children?' He would always bring it back to that one simple but vital motive. What a legend of a man.

When I am doing the Rickshaw Challenge, I never feel the need to hassle people for a donation. It's not about putting on sad music or manipulating people to give money, nothing like that; it's all about celebrating where these youngsters are at in their lives, and how they are about to become brilliant young adults because of the support that they've had . . . it's that simple. Essentially, all I do is create a platform for the public to show their support.

And boy, have they showed their support!

One final word on this incredible experience: I always associate autumn weather with the Rickshaw Challenge, as I feel the change in temperature in my bones and I have flashbacks of big hills and Lycra!

# 7

# Birds and Mini-Beasts

Even though the farm is set in a beautiful part of the countryside, with berries and food aplenty, my dad is literally obsessed with looking after the wild birds that share our farm and valley with us. He supplement-feeds them all the time and spends a small fortune every year filling dozens and dozens of bird feeders in various places around the farm, every day, just to make sure they are all OK. He has huge sacks of bird feed delivered, and it sometimes takes him hours to refill every feeder!

We have a feeding station on the bank behind the house. It's like a wild aviary out of the kitchen window, constantly rammed with a huge variety of species. Dad has loads of feeders set up on branches, too. It's really lovely – you stand at the kitchen sink and you can watch dozens of fluttering birds coming in for a snack. Of course, some of the food drops to the floor, so there will always be loads of birds pecking away at the scraps, too. The whole area is always alive with feathered friends!

Dad has this amazing bird-feeding station that he sited in what we call our 'ging gang garden' (named after a big stone building with the horses in that used to grind the mill in that area). There is a line of protected pines along the one side that was planted purely to shelter the farm and the farmhouse from the prevailing winds, so the bird station enjoys decent protection (we also fixed a number of bat boxes up in these trees). Dad loves to sit in his caravan and watch all the birds so close by, and he will happily spend hours watching and photographing them all feeding.

We have done an enormous amount of work on the farm to attract and accommodate a number of rare bird species, too. There is a registered 'red list' of birds to be concerned about that we try to help. A good example would be tree sparrows (sometimes known as 'little vicars', due to their white collars). These birds are different to the house sparrow that we are all familiar with, because they are smaller and more active, and their tail is often cocked.

In recent times, there has been a massive decline in the population of tree sparrows, with some estimates suggesting a drop of over 90 per cent from their peak. Dad has worked hard to make the farm attractive to this species and I am delighted to say they are in abundance here now. You do this by introducing certain plants into your hedges that the tree sparrow is known to like, you provide certain food sources and so on, you basically create the perfect environment for them to thrive – but ultimately, after that you are in the hands of Mother Nature as to whether the intended new guests will arrive. When they do, I find it incredibly humbling and rewarding. However, farmers will be faced with the issue of 'Do I feed the nation or do I feed our wildlife?' and that is a very real dilemma. I would never say to anybody, 'You need to do this on your farm,' I'm just not that kind of person. Speaking personally and just for our farm, we try to support and encourage these birds that need our help here.

We've also been encouraging barn owls on the farm. I made two breed-specific nesting boxes and sited them in trees that are opposite each other across a field, so that the owls can see one another. These much-loved owls roost separately, with the male in one tree and the female in the other. The chicks will be raised in one box and the male will sit and guard from across in his box. The young tend to make loud calls begging for food, so it is preferable that we provide boxes in close proximity and easily accessible to each parent.

Barn owls really are amazing birds – I occasionally see them during the day and every time I do, it stops me in my tracks. Their colouring in daylight is so striking, but also they have unbelievable charisma, this aura, as they fly through the valley. They seem to own the airspace that they are in – I often see them out hunting if I am driving along the track late at night with the headlights on, so graceful, so silent.

A barn owl's preferred meal is a small mammal, such as a mouse or a field vole – unfortunately for these little furry fellows, a barn owl is able to fly almost silently when it is on the hunt, so they will likely have no idea they are about to be a night-time meal until it is too late. These owls have incredibly sensitive hearing and can sense the tiniest of movements out in the fields, even in very poor light. When they are moving in for a meal, they rely on their hearing and then use the comb-like fringed edges of their feathers to swoop down on their prey in silence. A downside of this predatory asset is that the feathers are not particularly waterproof, so particularly wet and foul weather can be a challenge for barn owls, not least because if they get soaked, they cannot hunt and will therefore go hungry. So our owl boxes hopefully offer them some welcome shelter where they can stay dry. One final word on the owl boxes – barn owls will roost for up to twenty-two hours a day, so they definitely need somewhere to hang out!

We are also lucky enough to have grey herons in the valley, and when you see one flying past, the sheer size of their wingspan and their elegance is breathtaking, just mesmerizing to watch. Other natural birds on or around our farm include lapwings, curlews, yellowhammers, yellow wagtails, wrens, woodpeckers (both lesser and greater spotted as well as green), siskins, nuthatches, redstarts, mistle thrushes, cuckoos, skylarks, swallows, swifts, buzzards and, more recently, red kites. We did have a visiting hoopoe, which was unbelievable: that's a bird often found across much of Africa and Asia, but it sort of got lost and somehow ended up on our farm track! My dad grabbed his long lens and managed to get a photo of it, which was incredible. We've also got dunnocks, bramblings, pheasants, blue tits, great tits, coal tits, long-tailed tits, pied wagtails, tawny owls, loads of doves, treecreepers, rooks, crows, jays and magpies, red-legged partridges and blackbirds!

We've also got house martins that live in the valley and around the house. The National Trust tracked one of them to eastern Africa, and that same bird comes back to our farmhouse every year. Of all the places in the world, they choose to return to our farm. When I look up into the sky and see those house martins returning, when there is no one else around . . . we own that moment together; they're not frightened of me, they are happy to be back . . . the joy that feeling gives me is actually hard to put into words. I find it baffling HOW they do that – flying from thousands of miles away . . . I sometimes see them overhead and imagine they might be looking down, thinking, *Ah, yes, there's the Bakers' – this must be our stop!*

We've got all sorts of chickens that run about on the farm. Aside from the egg-laying breeds that we have, the family has also been very successful breeding a number of more ornamental birds. For example, we have some beautiful 'Silkies'. These are quite amazing birds, because they are black-skinned, they are black-muscled and they even have black bones (black eyes, too!). They also have an extra toe – normally chickens have four toes, but Silkies have one extra. They are amazing-looking birds, with an almost cartoon-like 'pom pom' appearance to their heads. Their feathers are more like fur, to be honest, and that's actually where Mum first saw them – in an aptly named 'Fur and Feather' tent at an agricultural show. This plumage is the main reason my mum was attracted to them in the first place. Biologically, their feathers don't have any barbicels, which are the little hooks that tend to hold feathers together tightly, so this is why they look so fluffy. The downside of this for our lovely Silkies is that they can't fly and aren't waterproof.

It is widely believed that Silkies are Chinese in origin, possibly dating back as far as 206 BC, which is why some breeders even refer to them as Chinese Silkies. In fact, the Chinese name for them is *wu-gu-ji*, which means 'black-boned'. According to the Happy Chicken Coop website, the explorer Marco

Polo even came back from his travels around the Far East in the thirteenth century and told people about seeing a 'furry chicken'. Later descriptions in Italian literature detail a chicken with 'fur like a black cat'. Silkies are often referred to as 'the ultimate in kids' chickens' because they are so very gentle-natured. They also make great mothers.

There is a fine art to pampering these chickens because, and this is quite hilarious really, their feathers react perfectly to a hairdryer! If they get wet, they can look quite comically drenched, but a gentle drying with the hairdryer soon has them looking all fluffy again (it isn't good for them to get wet, so it's important to dry them off quickly). There are many events for showing chickens such as Silkies and it can get very competitive. My mum is an expert, she can get the old hairdryer out, fluff them up and make them look like real prima donnas! She sometimes uses talcum powder to make them whiter. I tell you something, chicken grooming is a dark art!

We also breed Seramas and Pekins. Seramas are actually the smallest chickens in the world – they range in height from ten inches down to as little as six! Their eggs are so small that you would need five to get the same size omelette as a normal laying hen's egg. The very smallest females might only weigh as little as eight ounces, so these really are very tiny birds. They originated in Malaysia and to this day are very popular in Singapore. Although they are still relatively rare in the UK, they are my favourites, they are so well proportioned, beautiful and dainty. Luke is a huge fan, and in fact he now breeds Seramas. If you saw a picture of a Pekin, you wouldn't realize how small they are because they're so perfectly proportioned. You can hold one on your hand and see up close how they have the most perfect dimensions. They are really sociable, and Luke will think nothing of popping one on his shoulder – they're really good company. The Pekins (and Silkies) have feathery feet! The feathers run down their legs and over their feet so they look very distinctive.

We also have some Pencil Wyandottes, which I always think look very sort of art deco – if a chicken can look art deco, that is! I say that because these American chickens have this beautiful 1920s design to their plumage: they are so beautiful. Sometimes their plumes almost look like a high-society gentleman's smart herringbone suit; they really are very striking.

The breeds such as Silkies are less productive in the egg department, and you might only get three a week, whereas a laying breed might produce one a day. You know when they are laying because you hear them clucking away! We've got a helter-skelter for all our eggs in the kitchen, because they can stack up pretty quickly. It's a fun way to store them all, but the little Silkies' eggs are so small that they fall through the rails!

The Silkies don't exactly eat much food, so they are relatively economical to look after. These birds prefer to strut around looking beautiful and socializing with us! They are a very entertaining addition to have wandering around the farm. In fact, some of these breeds, such as the Seramas, are actually used as therapy chickens. Our chickens have a similar existence to the one that I used to have on *The One Show* – free-ranging, wild during the day, getting covered in mud, out in the elements, loving it, and then they get preened and fussed over and spruced up, ready to go on show!

If this all sounds very idyllic, then let me tell you, there is a downside to letting your free-range chickens roam around all over the farm – specifically when you grab a hay bale and find out that they've been sitting on the top and doing their business. You soon find out about any evidence!

Looking after the chickens in wintertime can be very time-consuming. When there are bird flu outbreaks, you need to keep your chickens away from the droppings of any potentially infected birds that may be flying overhead, so during any outbreak you need to keep them sheltered and covered over. You will also have the chickens' food and water undercover, so no wild birds can access the supplies and potentially contaminate our farm birds. It can be a challenge, keeping free-roaming chickens away from any bird poo across a hundred acres, but it's really vital that we do. If there is an outbreak, the government is able to analyse and offer the correct advice, and we are very stringent with those rules and stick to the letter.

There is another very severe threat to chickens for any farmer, us included: foxes. If a fox gets inside a hen house, it will be carnage. They will kill chickens for fun – it is a killing frenzy – and they will attack everything that moves in the coop.

With an ever-increasing flock size, we often use an incubator that turns the eggs and is kept at a constant thirty-eight degrees. You add some water to make sure you have got the right humidity and then you increase that as the eggs develop further. You can check up on each egg to see if there is life inside by doing what is called 'candling' – you literally shine a light underneath them and you can tell from the shadows if everything is still OK inside the shell. It is fascinating to watch: you can follow the blood vessels developing inside as the chick grows. You incubate for twenty-one days and then these tiny chicks peck their way out. You put them straight under a heat plate to keep them warm, which you do all together, because they also keep each other warm. Then you sit back and watch as they grow very, very quickly! The rate at which birds grow is so incredibly rapid, it is shocking to see, so within days they look less like tiny chicks and more like little birds. I love it when we have chicks hatching; it is just a wonder to witness.

We had a male peacock on the farm for seventeen years – we didn't buy him, he just sort of wandered up the track one day! The neighbouring farm used to rear them and one day this peacock decided that he wanted to come and live with us, which we obviously had no problems with. He had this beautiful dark azure blue on his chest that used to shine in the light, especially if he was roosting on the roof of the byre, the single-storey building that adjoins the farmhouse. He had these great big wings and when he flapped them to roost up there, you could hear this amazing whooshing sound. He really looked after himself, he did his own thing, but he was quite noisy; you'd hear him a lot – he used to shout all the time. He had this unbelievably loud call that used to echo around the valley. If he wasn't roosting, he'd be sunning himself on the lawn in the sunshine. He was so magnificent; I used to love that you'd just be walking around the farm, going about your business, and you'd suddenly come across a beautiful peacock feather. We could never work out if it was supposed to be good or bad luck to take peacock feathers inside – but we did anyway, and put them in a long, waist-height vase. Then, after a while, we decided it might be bad luck after all, so we took the feathers outside and spent the next few weeks trying to decide if our life had got better or not! That peacock was a beauty.

We also have loads of red-legged partridges: they sort of use our farm road as an athletics track. You feel awful when you are driving up the track, because they never get out of your way and have to run the whole length of the track, three-quarters of a mile, before they dive off to safety. I don't want to call them stupid birds but they're not exactly brains of Britain. Luckily, we haven't run any over yet.

We also have hundreds of pheasants. They like to hang around Dad's bird-feeding stations and pick up the scraps of seeds that fall to the floor. We have actual pheasant feeders as well, which are a blue barrel up on three legs, with a hole in the bottom with a spring attached. You fill up the barrel with seed, the birds peck around this central metal spring and the feed drops down on to the floor. It fattens them up incredibly well. Even though they are fattened up, we never eat the pheasants, we let them live out their natural life, which can actually be quite a long time for some of them (their average life expectancy in the wild can be as little as a year). People often think pheasants must be really slow because, sadly, you do see a lot having been run over, but actually their top speed in flight can be as high as 60 mph if they are being chased!

Our ancient woodland is a really old roosting site for all of the crows, rooks and jackdaws from right across the valley and the Dales. On an evening – I've grown up with this sound – all these crows are calling in unison, it is very hard to describe how that feels when you hear it, it's almost like the heartbeat of the woods, a natural Mexican wave at your favourite concert venue.

There is a rookery in the ancient woodland and we are lucky enough to get 'murmurations' of rooks – these are huge formations of birds that twist, swoop and swirl across the sky seemingly in perfect unison, like beautiful shape-shifting clouds. This tends to happen just before dusk, above a specific communal roosting site which, in our case, is the woodland. Right below the farm, it is an astonishing sight and the first time you see one, it takes your breath away – in fact, it does every time I see one. It's almost like this alien form in the sky. We get these pulsating groups of rooks that come through and whip round the farmhouse, then go off and swoop between the two oak trees – one by the house and the other at the corner of the farm track – and you just get engulfed. It really is a phenomenal thing to witness. Experts believe that these murmurations offer safety in numbers. Believe it or not, the largest recorded murmuration was of starlings in Somerset, and was said to contain over six million birds! However, even the experts don't know for certain how each bird is able to follow the rest without bumping into one another. One theory is that they follow the six or so birds nearest to each other, and that creates this aerial mimicry in terms of their rippling formation – but we don't know definitively. That just adds to the magic and the mystery.

If you are lucky enough to be down in the ancient woodlands when our murmurations of rooks happen, it is incredible. I believe that it is more rare for rooks than starlings to behave like this, which adds to that special feeling of being surrounded by thousands of birds, dancing in the sky in this ritual of perfect harmony, above all these oaks and other trees that have been here for centuries . . . wow!

Crows have a fairly mixed reputation, I think it is fair to say. The ones who live in our woodlands have been known to attack – and in some cases blind – our sheep. Believe it or not, the crows are also the biggest threat to our lambs – as carrion feeders, they are attracted to the afterbirth. If you've got a newly born lamb struggling to find its feet in the field a few minutes after being born, the crows will swoop down and peck at the afterbirth, and because the lamb is still covered in that, it can very easily be hurt or killed. That's what happened to one lamb they blinded that still wanders around the farm today. We can't eradicate crows from our farm, they are native and part of the food chain, so we just have to manage them in a way that is helpful to our livestock and sympathetic to the natural way of life.

Moving further down the food chain, let's talk about insects and smaller creatures, which I like to call 'mini-beasts', a term that has always made me smile. I am fascinated by the insect world, because whenever you lift up a stone or piece of wood, or move a feed bag that has been on the ground for a long time, you are just transported to this other world where all these tiny inhabitants are so busy and so determined. I don't want to be too anthropomorphic about it, but you never imagine them having a day off or just sort of sitting and relaxing. The insect world is full on!

Mini-beasts are an important food source for animals such as birds and bats, but they also help to pollinate flowering plants and crops. They also act as predators to small insects such as aphids. Their busy lives will also help with soil decomposition and enrich the soil around us. In fact, 80 per cent of UK plants are pollinated by insects, while others help break down plants and animals, making them an absolutely vital part of our ecosystem.

My favourite mini-beast is actually the woodlouse. Very common, of course, but off-the-scale amazing. They feed off dead plants and creatures, which in turn recycles these elements and helps return vital nutrients into the environment. There are around thirty-five to forty species of woodlouse in the UK, which range in colour from brown to grey and even pink! They are actually crustaceans, related to crabs, shrimps and lobsters, which in fact makes them one of the very few land-based crustaceans. They have gills near the back legs, which they use to breathe, but also to draw dampness and oxygen from the air. That is why you will find them in places like under rotting wood. That blows my mind.

And who can forget the beautiful ladybird? This species is, in fact, a type of beetle. Their easily recognizable bright red wing cases with black spots have featured in a thousand children's picture books, and must be one of our most cherished British insects. Most common are the seven-spot variety, but all ladybirds' colourings are intended to warn predators that they taste very bitter! To other, hostile mini-beasts, ladybirds also give off a pungent smell, by way of deterrent.

Butterflies are very useful and important pollinators and obviously very beautiful to look at. Amazingly, they can live as little as a week or up to as long as a year, depending on the species. They have some frankly mind-boggling traits, too – for example, their four wings (not two) are transparent, and it is actually pigments on modified hairs (known as scales) over the wing that reflect light in different ways and create the splashes of colour that are

so breathtaking. Also, butterflies taste with their feet and they can't fly if they get cold! The long, protruding proboscis that you can see on their head is how they drink; in fact, they don't actually eat at all, they just use their proboscis to take in nectar, rotten fruit, water from puddles or even to suck on dead animals!

I love worms, too, which are invertebrates rather than insects. Their role in recycling dead plants, fallen leaves, bacteria and dead animals is essential, and because some types of worm can actually eat up to their own body weight in food every day, they are very productive and useful little creatures. The little curly mounds you see across lawns are called casts and are the end result of this recycling process – in other words, that's worm poo! In doing this job, worms help to insert nitrates, phosphorus and bacteria back into the soil. They also loosen and oxygenate the soil as they burrow and dig down, all of which helps to improve the soil's structure and quality.

Next time you see a worm wriggling about, just remember: they are the key to the future of our food production, which in turn means that they are one of the most important organisms that we have on the earth.

With regards to insects, as I've said earlier, look after the little creatures and the rest will take care of themselves – so we are always finding ways to make their environment around the farm more appealing, from log piles in the woodland to up around the ging gang area, where we planted ten thousand wild flowers. You can research species-specific flora and plant those, then sit back and see what decides to move in. We are obviously very fortunate to have a lot of space at the farm, so we can plant a large quantity of wild flowers that will give insects a great chance to thrive. The added benefit for us is that the area will be filled with vibrant colours, so it looks amazing, but will be very much a wild garden, rather than anything more formal. Even if you don't have a garden, there are plants you can use in a window box that will attract bees and other flying insects, butterflies, all sorts – it's really marvellous. Regardless of scale, the key is that wild flowers will help create this place where insects thrive and everything benefits.

Everything's got to live somewhere.

# 8

# Winter

Winter on our farm can be brutal, there's no way of dressing that up. The cold is kind of indescribable, really, and much of that is to do with the wind and the very low temperatures travelling down through the valley. It can get savagely cold and that's when you'll hear us say, 'I am nithered!' – when it's so cold that it goes through into your bones and you just can't get warm. But then again, that is also the joy of a roaring fire.

Due to the position of the farmhouse, you can often watch the severe weather come down the valley – it can be raining in the bottom field but not by the farmhouse and you can stand outside and watch it go across below you; it is quite amazing really. And at least the winters are so harsh that they make you really appreciate the beauty of spring and the warmth of the summer!

In terms of looking after the animals and the farm during the cold months, much of winter is about preparation. Getting ready for bad weather, obviously, but also preparing for the spring when everything wants to burst back into life. When the bad weather is heading our way, the first thing I think is, *Have we got enough gas? Have we got enough supplies if we are snowed in?* We are lucky enough to have a lovely big walk-in pantry, which is the heart of the home. In the summertime, this pantry keeps everything cool, and in the wintertime it is like walking into your very own corner shop. In the pantry there are shelves and racks of food with big slabs of stone on the top that the food can sit on and still feel refrigerated. There are red-and-white-checked gingham covers on the shelves, which are filled with jars of preserves: it is basically heaven.

An important job in early winter is maintaining the farm buildings, shelters and pens. On any farm,

keeping buildings and shelters watertight is key, but
in a place as exposed to extreme weather as ours,
it is vital and never-ending. Things can take quite
a battering up here, so you always keep an eye out
for prevention. I regularly walk around the farm,
looking for problems that are about to arise: a loose
tile that has started to slip, a piece of guttering that
is getting blocked, shelters that are starting to leak.
We've repointed all the stonework on the front of
the house and on the barns, because the weather can
really cause things to perish, and before you know
it, you have a massive rebuild on your hands. This is
just a much more efficient way to work – if you spot
the problem beforehand and actually do something
about it, then it's so much less work than waiting

until there has been some big incident. Simple but effective: just keep on top of stuff. I also enjoy giving something a longer lifespan, so with the odd little repairs that you do around the farm, it just means that everything lasts a lot longer.

You may have guessed from all the stories of my dad returning from auctions with a truck full of entire school gymnasiums that he is something of a collector. He loves to keep all sorts of interesting items, bits and bats. He loves craftsmanship and anything that has been made well – but also he hates waste. Over the years, he has collected a huge amount of wood in the barn. You go in there and it's like a timber merchant's; there's always a piece of wood knocking about that will get you started. I love diving in there, rummaging around for a piece of timber, then coming out and starting to fashion that wood into exactly what I need. It is also a lot cheaper than going out and buying it new.

Best of all, you get a sense of personal satisfaction when you look at something being used and know that you've built that yourself. A classic example are the bat and bird boxes that I have built with Dad. Some days we lose ourselves in the barn for hours, sifting through all these old off-cuts, then start to build a bat or bird box; it's extremely relaxing and we have a lovely time together.

The bats on the farm are really interesting and we actively encourage them. They are an important part of the biodiversity of any farm. There are eighteen species of bats in the UK, which make up a quarter of our mammal species, but we aren't certain yet what species of bats live on our farm. Even so, it's fantastic that some of them choose to live with us. We often stand out at twilight and see the bats swooping around the farmhouse; we even have a bat detector which helps you pick up on any activity and listen in on the bats talking to each other. Fascinating.

Many bats in the UK prefer to roost in trees. Where trees are not available or ideal, then they will look to nest in man-made bat boxes. The trees offer the bats food in the form of insects and obviously shelter. A bat will often have its young in the higher parts of a tree's canopy, but then move lower down for hibernation in the winter.

Bat populations have suffered a terrible decline in the past hundred years or so, making it even more vital that we provide a welcoming and hospitable environment for them to settle and breed on the farm. When you see a bat or bird fly into a box that you've made, then watch over the weeks as it raises its young and they eventually fly off, then watch still further as they all return every year – because they like living here – well, it's just great. I get a lot of satisfaction out of seeing that.

It helps that I have a massive array of tools for pretty much any job that crops up. Ever since I was a young lad – and still to this day – my dad has always bought me tools. Every Christmas, every birthday, that's what he buys me, and I love it; I've got a great collection! Drill bits on angles that go round corners, so many different saws, traditional chisels, socket sets, every conceivable type of hammer and screwdriver, you name it. I get quite geeky about tools – so, for example, I am a big fan of a Japanese pull saw. In case you are not, these are saws with teeth in reverse, so they cut on the pull, not the push like conventional saws. You can't have too many Japanese pull saws!

During winter, we do get snowed in fairly regularly. The valley acts as a wind tunnel, and when it snows the wind whips it all up so that it collects in huge piles right across the farm. When I was at school, being blocked in by snow was always the perfect excuse not to go in, because sometimes I literally couldn't get out of our front door. There have been extreme occasions when the snow drifts have reached up to the first-floor windows and a couple of times I have even climbed out of my bedroom window and slid down the snow drift to the doorstep below.

If we do get snowed in, the farm track can some-times become impassable. It is around three-quarters of a mile long, and at least once a year we have to dig it out with a JCB. I love it when the snow is like that; as much as it is practically very challenging, at the same time it is completely mesmerizing. There's something about waking up to extreme snow that brings out the adventurer in me!

There's actually only been one time when we were so fully snowed in that we were unable to make it away from the farm. I had a really important few days lined up filming *Blue Peter*, but this huge snow-storm completely blocked us in. I was determined to get down to London, so we shovelled the snow away from my car — which was just a two-wheel-drive Fiat Brava — then I jumped in alongside Nicola and drove like some kind of obsessed Olympic skier down across the fields. I was literally skating my car across several feet of snow on these unnervingly steep slopes, Nicola was holding on to the dashboard like some white-knuckle bobsleigh ride . . . I have no idea how my car survived, but it did an amazing job! We eventually made it down through all the fields to the road at the bottom in one piece — I tell you something, the sense of achievement when we hit the main road was class — we were over the moon! Some hours later, we made it to the BBC and it felt like some madcap expedition that should've been on *Blue Peter*, rather than just me getting to work!

Of course, as much as the schoolboy in me loves to wake up to snow, not all the animals do. It can be very serious for certain, less hardy breeds if we are caught off guard. The Hampshires need to be in, under cover and sheltered, otherwise it can get dangerous for them very quickly. Necessarily, we have built some field shelters which give them the option to wander in for protection if we haven't reacted as quickly as we would like, for whatever reason. With the new, hardier breeds that we brought in after Mum's accident, we don't have to do so much of that.

For us, the worst part of the winter is actually after the snow has gone and you are just left with mud everywhere. It's slushy and sludgy, you can't walk anywhere without your boots getting stuck, it takes an age to do anything and you look at the ground and think, *How on earth is the land ever going to repair itself?* Yet it does, year after year; it comes back and that's what I love.

When I was younger, in the lead-up to Christmas, Nicola and myself used to do a holly harvest from the woodland every year. Mum and Dad said, 'Whatever you can cut and sell, it's yours,' so we would go and get bin liners and just be lopping and chopping and stuffing these bags full of all this beautiful berried holly. Then we would fill the cattle trailer with our harvest and go off to the local markets such as at Chester-le-Street, Durham and Darlington. We made a few quid actually!

Christmas on the farm is all about food, really. Mum is a fantastic cook, and she makes the most unbelievable Christmas dinner. Actually, that's not just on Christmas Day, it's the whole festive season really; there is a lot of food and the beautiful aromas that come out of the kitchen are just incredible.

Outside on Christmas Eve, we go around the farm stuffing the feeders to the gunnels, so that we have a little extra time on Christmas morning before we have to venture out and replenish the animals' food. If you get it right, you can open all the presents and cards first, before heading out.

I love to finish filling all the feeders on Christmas Eve and then just take a moment to look at the stars – the light pollution up here is zero, the sky is pitch black and the stars twinkle in the most enchanting way. You usually only have to wait a few minutes before you see a shooting star. As a boy, I used to stare for hours and hours looking for Santa flying across the sky and I've never forgotten that feeling. Imagining the Three Wise Men navigating by the stars and the feeling that when you look up, you could be in any country in any century . . . it's timeless. The view up there hasn't changed at all. A few years ago, we bought Dad a telescope for Christmas and we've watched all sorts, from the Northern Lights to the space station.

We have some lovely traditions inside the farmhouse, too. In terms of a Christmas tree, we take one from the row of trees that are planted along the right-hand side of the farm (to shelter it from the wind). Sometimes we lop the top off a really tall tree just to get the little triangular tip, but usually Mum picks a massive tree and we have to somehow find a way to ram it inside the lounge! Most years it will need to be trimmed and fashioned to fit into the alcove in the corner. Every year Mum adorns the house with so much stuff that my dad always spends the day keeping out of the way until it's all finished. As soon as the Christmas decorations are coming out, it is so chaotic, there are garlands hanging from the chimney breasts, there are all sorts of decorations that have been collected through the years that tell the story of our family through the generations.

Every year my dad writes my mum a Christmas card that he gave her the first year that I was born . . . and every year he writes a new paragraph summing up what has happened in the last twelve months. It's a musical card and I love that moment when my dad brings the card down. Mum winds up the little chrome handle and it plays the music while she reads it and it is always emotional to look back at what's happened as a family over the years. It's a fabulous tradition.

Once we have opened the presents and cards, it's straight outside to feed all the animals. I love feeding up on Christmas Day because if you are out and it's cold, you know that when you get back in, there will be a roaring fire on. Throughout the whole of Christmas there is a log fire going, it's just this continual blaze, every morning the embers of last night's fire will be started afresh for the coming day.

You come back into the warm, and eat loads of beautiful food. Mum does turkey, pies and potatoes every single way you can imagine, she does a 'broccoli mousse' which is one of my favourites, mountains of stuffings, every single veg you can think of, she does a Beef Wellington, left-over turkey curries . . . it's all so delicious!

At Christmas, I also get this slightly weird clash of my two worlds colliding: I will be sitting relaxing in the farmhouse, all nice and warm by the fire, having gone out and fed up, then I look at what is on the telly. We have a family tradition of going through the *Radio Times* to see what is on during the festive period, and often see programmes that I have made.

I find myself sitting there, looking at a picture of me – it always feels a bit odd!

One of my absolute favourite winter jobs is drystone walling. As well as the wonderfully rich ecosystems of hedgerows, our farm is blessed with some magnificent drystone walls on various borders (as a generalization, hedgerows are more likely to be found in the lowland regions, while drystone walls are often used in uplands). Although you can obviously do drystone walling at any time of the year, for a number of reasons it is ideally a job for winter, ready for the spring and summertime. You know you are not going to be busy with the haymaking or any demanding schedules like that, plus if you crack on at this time, you know that your walls are going to be ready and sturdy for the heavier winter that is to come. It also helps that you don't have to wade through waist-high grass or nettles to do the work!

Even though I have been around drystone walls for pretty much all of my life, they still amaze me. The name gives the game away – these are stone walls made without any mortar or other compounds to knit them together. They can be traced back thousands of years – according to some sources, the earliest variants, using mounds of soil and large boulders, arguably go back as far as the Iron Age or in some cases even earlier. In the UK, they have been built for generations, shaping and hemming in our countryside and farmland with such simple and efficient elegance. Drystone walls enjoyed their first burst of popularity in the post-medieval years when much of the country moved out of sharing areas of 'common land' and increasing numbers of land-owners wanted to enclose their own fields.

Originally, the walls would have been constructed using stone that was easily to hand and sourced locally, making it a practical and accessible way to make boundaries. That said, the process of sourcing the stone centuries ago would've still been incredibly labour-intensive, involving digging by hand and dragging the boulders and rocks on horse-drawn sledges across fields and dirt tracks.

In case you are wondering how a stone wall with no mortar stays up, it is all to do with the construction technique. In essence, they are actually two walls, with filler pieces inside called 'heart stones'. This creates a triangle-like formation, where the two walls are almost leaning into each other, which is what gives the wall its strength. The specific way they are interlocked means you don't use any mortar or soil yet they are so, so strong. There is nothing in there other than the stones themselves, these tiny little heart stones wedged in and the occasional 'through stone' to bind the two sides together. Then on the top are what's known as 'coping stones', which weigh down on the wall and hold it all together. Some walls have openings for smaller livestock to pass through, which we call 'sheep creeps'.

Making drystone walls in this way has been tried and tested over thousands of years and, even more impressively, some of these walls are believed to date back millennia. Part of this longevity is the fact that the construction method allows the walls to move and adjust to prevailing weather conditions, such as harsh winds or battering rain.

My mind boggles when I see the countless miles of these remarkably durable drystone walls across the UK, because it is such an incredibly labour-intensive process. Building an average wall will typically take around a day for every three metres. There is a saying among drystone-wall builders that the ultimate disappointment is if a wall you made falls down in your lifetime. Personally, I find drystone walls totally fascinating and have to admit it is a satisfying job to do. Whenever I spend a day drystone walling, I find the entire process very therapeutic; it's incredibly distracting from whatever is on your mind, and ultimately very rewarding.

One aspect of drystone walls that I find interesting is the regional nature of the style and construction methods. Obviously, the type of stone that is readily available may differ from county to county – for example, sandstone, limestone or slate – but over the centuries, the type of construction has also differed from region to region. I have to admit – and I recognize this may be pretty niche! – I love a trip to the National Stone Centre, which is set in six former limestone quarries in the Derbyshire Dales, near the edge of the Peak District National Park. At the turn of this century, volunteers there built the Millennium Wall, which uses six-metre sections of the many different types of drystone walling styles and materials from around the UK. Brilliant!

Whenever I see drystone walls or work on them, I can't help thinking that they define how so much of Britain looks. The gloriously green patchwork that makes up our wonderful island is so often edged and framed by these walls, meticulously crafted and shaped over years and years by generations of skilled farmers and labourers. Certainly, if you are ever in a plane and lucky enough to fly low over drystone walls, it is a marvel to behold. Believe it or not, there are said to be over five thousand miles of drystone walling in Yorkshire alone, and enough in the UK to wrap five times around the world. They are so evocative of this country, so typical and, along with hedgerows, have drawn a boundary around our country life for thousands of years.

A nice touch that we did with one of the drystone walls at the farm was for a *Blue Peter* piece. Along with a good friend of mine, Michael, who is a brilliant waller, we were filming a feature about the tradition of drystone walls and showing how they were made. He explained that back in the day it was always the tradition that the wall builder would put in a trinket or something related to him, so that when (if) the wall eventually fell down, decades or even hundreds of years later, someone would find that little memento. It's like planting a piece of history, waiting to be found. So we thought, *Let's put a* Blue Peter *badge in there*, which was also in keeping with the show's long-standing tradition of burying time capsules.

So, at some point in the future, hopefully hundreds of years from now, if that wall finally crumbles, someone will find that badge . . .

One of the most life-enriching and rewarding elements of living and working on a farm like ours is the amazing characters you meet all the time. Let me tell you about a lovely fella that we call George the Bee Man (officially, he is a beekeeper!). A few years back, George got hold of some hives and he says he was obsessed with them straight away. He now has over 180 hives! He just instantly fell in love with bees

Nicola and me on our
wedding day. I'm so fortunate
to have married the most
beautiful and caring soul,
who somehow makes
everything happen.

Unsurprisingly, the church we
got married in had sheep
roaming in the churchyard!

Me, Lace and Meg as a pup off to feed up on the farm.

Here I am feeding up in the snow – this is an average sprinkling on the farm track.

I loved every minute of my career on *Blue Peter* . . .

Picking up Meg with my sheepdog mentor
Derek Bowmer.

One of our official *Blue Peter* postcards.

My *Blue Peter* heyday with Simon, Konnie and Liz. So many happy memories!

*Blue Peter* always found a way to challenge me . . .

Me on my tandem hang-gliding world record – safe to say it was an experience I'll never forget!

Another one of my many *Blue Peter* challenges – I was training with the paratroopers on the toughest obstacle course ever!

It has been a privilege to ride with every member of Team Rickshaw over ten years.

Travelling to the Atlas Mountains and meeting Ali Louche was one of my most memorable *Blue Peter* trips.

It's incredible what the Rickshaw Challenge has become. It's the highlight of my year and a great example of people power.

This palette-knife oil painting of Saint-Paul de Vence was the catalyst for me to get back into art.

This is the first painting I plucked up the courage to post on my Instagram.

A landscape valley I painted at a local art day.

and set about becoming the absolute expert that he is. When you talk to George you learn something new about bees or honey every time.

He is always looking for new places to put hives that might produce really rich honey. With our farm being organic and having ancient hay meadows, with all those species of flowers and plants that I've explained grow in both the meadows and hedgerows, George was very keen to talk to us about taking some hives. In return, we loved the idea of offering his bees a place to work.

We started with six hives in the corner of the top hay field on the right-hand side of the main farm track. It's a new venture for us and we are really excited to see how that develops. The idea of eating honey that has been made on our own farm is so exciting to me. George's wife makes candles and all sorts of crafty stuff, too, so there are a wide number of products that you can make. George has explained to me about all the different types of honey and he says he will take me up to the moorland one day to harvest this very special type of honey you can get when the heather starts to flower for the first time; apparently it has this pollen that produces an unbelievable taste.

It's fascinating watching George at work. I filmed him for our TV show *Our Farm in the Dales* and it was a joy to help him release his bees. His enthusiasm and energy are infectious. He dropped the bees off at the back end of winter, which is really the best time to move them. They almost relocate themselves as they start to venture out in spring and begin to look around and get their new coordinates. George said they come out of their hives after relocation and do a figure of eight to get their bearings; he also said they can fly up to three miles away from the hive and come back again like clockwork. Bees are an incredibly community-focused species. Their entire existence revolves around the hive, the queen, their community.

According to the Woodland Trust, there are more than 250 species of bee in the UK, including bumble-bees, mason bees and even mining bees! There are twenty-four types of bumblebee in the UK, which is why we all know them so well. Mason bees are called that because of their preference for living around bricks and rocks, often nesting in cavities in walls or wood. Mining bees are even more curious; this solitary species burrows into the ground, hence the name! As for the good old honeybee, we only have one type in the UK: they're slim with a black abdomen and golden-amber bands circling around them. George is part of a very long heritage of people working with these bees – they have been domesticated for centuries, so much so that truly wild colonies are pretty rare. Although bumblebees tend to have small hives of only a few hundred bees or so, honeybees are much more sociable, so a typical hive will contain around twenty to thirty thousand bees. They particularly enjoy living near willows, orchard trees, oilseed rape, raspberry flowers and other trees, herbs and shrubs.

The bee population has been declining alarmingly, so it is vital that people such as George continue to help stop this worrying trend. We can all help by planting a diverse range of mini-beast-friendly flowers that are rich in pollen-covered, nectar-rich species. 'Bug hotels' are also great: you can make these yourself from old bits of wood, and items you find around the garden, such as sticks, pine cones, conkers and suchlike.

When we first got the hives, I was full of hundreds of questions for George. I was fascinated by what the bees do in the hive at different times of year. For example, during the colder winter months, when they spend all their time in the hives, I was amazed to discover that they actually regulate the temperature of the hive by contracting their muscles in a certain way to actually vibrate their bodies, which in turn warms up the inside of the hive! Quite incredible.

If it is too hot in there, their solution is even more ingenious, and we only found out one day when I was watching these bees by an old pig feeder in the farmyard which resembles a Mexican sombrero, with a peak on top and this doughnut-shaped circular tray round the middle where you pour the feed for the pigs to root around and eat. Over time, this had filled with rainwater, and then a few bits of grass must've fallen in there when we were strimming nearby, as it had piles of fermented grass in there too, like a little beach. Anyway, one day, I noticed hundreds of bees were all around this old feeder, and I also spotted that they looked inflated, certainly bigger than usual. We phoned George and asked him what was going on and he explained that they were literally filling themselves up with water, like stripey little flasks, then zooming off back home where they would use the water to cool the hive down. Just remarkable. The whole world of bees is just completely absorbing, and I can entirely see how George has come to be obsessed with them!

Of course, it isn't just about the hives and honey – it never ceases to amaze me just how helpful bees are with all the vegetation and plant species around the farm. Moving forward, now that we have these hives, I am fascinated to see what happens in the future, specifically if there is a notable impact on the landscape in terms of more flowers and pollination. Even across at the orchard, they may have an impact with regards to pollination of different apple varieties. Some apple species self-pollinate but some need our bees. That is a lovely connection between the bee community that we've got and the orchard: they will be busy pollinating the trees that we have put in for my dad. Once again, I find it really rewarding to introduce something new to the farm, create an opportunity for something to live here and grow and flourish, then just sit back and see what happens. I love having the bees here and it is going to be wonderful to watch them settle in and, I would imagine, make a huge difference.

While we are on the subject of honey, I am reminded of the time I went to the Ngorongoro crater in Tanzania with the Hadzabe tribe, whose currency is . . . you guessed it: honey. They have these huge baobab trees, and inside the hollows within the trunk the bees create the most amazing wild hives, which are huge and incredibly intricate. The tribal members would literally stick their arms inside these trunks, right into the middle of the honeycomb, and pull it out. They were massive and this guy I was with just went in there, no protection other than a smoking twig, and pulled all the honey out. I remember laughing because I had worn a flowered shirt that day, this brown Hawaiian shirt with all these bright blossoms on, and as I saw all these thousands of bees escaping from this tree, I was thinking, *I couldn't have worn a more inappropriate shirt for today!*

We also went out hunting and they gave me a bow and arrow made entirely from the trees and wood around the forest where they lived. They each had a particular arrow, which they'd carve their signature on to, and rub that with soil so you could see the markings. The purpose was to identify who had fired which arrow. Then, when they went hunting for food, whoever's arrow was closest to the heart of the animal that had been hit would get the best cuts of the meat for their family.

As we walked back to camp, they were firing at birds, collecting them up and hanging them from their belts, ready to cook on the fire for the night's dinner. After all, we may have been filming but, for them, every trip out was an opportunity to collect food.

When you live on a farm like ours, or any farm for that matter, one job that you can't ever miss, and one that takes time out of each and every day, is to feed up. At different times of the year, the feed requirements are different, but certainly winter requires you to be extremely vigilant. Let's face it, you can't say, *It's a bit wet and cold, I will do that tomorrow!* Whatever the weather – rain, snow, gales – you have got no choice. First thing in the morning and last thing at night, the animals are relying on you to feed up!

We have sheep feed pellets delivered in twenty-five-kilo sacks but first you have to get this bloomin' thing open. Now, my mum uses a knife or a pair of scissors; Nicola likes to get her nails in and has this knack of just threading the string out in the correct way so that it all comes off beautifully smoothly. I can't be doing with that; I dive in and tear off the plastic top but invariably I'll rip it at the wrong angle and spend ages collecting the feed that's strewn all over the floor.

Once the sack is open, our technique is for someone to drive along in the 4 × 4 with me sitting in the back, and I will drop these little piles of feed in certain places for the sheep. Ideally, you want each sheep to be able to run to its own little pile, or only one or two sheep per pile: you want to reduce the amount of competition for the feed, especially if the sheep are in lamb – you don't want them pushing up against each other. I've got a technique like a see-saw motion. I love it, because you can make whatever pattern you want with the sheep – sometimes we try and spell out words. We even tried to write 'Happy Birthday' one year for Mum but we only got to the letter 'B' and then ran out of feed! We also have hay racks, which are wheeled feeders that are low enough to disperse the hay through a mesh direct to the sheep, keeping it dry and off the ground.

We also feed them big round bales, the equivalent of delivering ten small square bales in one go. The different breeds get through them at different rates depending on how greedy they are. You could be putting a bale out a week for your Hampshires in the coldest time of year, but then something like the Herdwicks will be much less needy. (We also have what are called 'ring feeders' which are designed to stop the sheep clambering all over the round bales of hay.)

In the winter months, a lot of your time is spent in transit, moving from one field to another to check up on your stock and obviously to-ing and fro-ing with the feed from the hay barn or from the feed store to the fields. A complication for us is that as an organic farm we can't just spread our hay out all over the fields wherever we want, because that would stifle any growth underneath – the last thing you want to do is layer up hay on top of precious species. So you have to have designated feeding areas which are all mapped out on the organic plan, as part of our system.

Usually, our chickens get a type of hard, bagged feed called layers pellets. These cause less waste as they are very easy for the chickens to eat. The chicks have crumb but the adult birds have pellets, as well as a bit of corn as a treat. If you were to give them crumb instead – a finer form of chicken feed – there would be a lot of food wasted.

And last, but most definitely not least, you have to provide clean, abundant drinking water. It might sound like stating the obvious, but getting water to all your animals is so vital. All the water troughs freeze frequently during a cold spell, so you have to take fresh water around almost constantly. I remember that job as a kid: it would be biting outside and I'd have to haul these five-gallon drums on to the back of the quad and go round refilling all the water troughs. It used to be so cold that I had to wrap tracksuit bottoms around my head like a hat and then use the legs as a scarf round my face with a slit for my eyes, just to try to somehow keep the cold at bay.

Sheep can deteriorate very quickly if they get dehydrated. With a hundred acres to look after, you really do need to know exactly where all your livestock are all the time, otherwise you can lose animals. The task is made trickier at our farm because there are no streams running through the site.

Of course, you can't go running on foot around a hundred acres of steep Durham valley slopes all the time; we do have machines but we have to use very low-impact vehicles such as quad bikes, which are nimble and extremely useful but don't damage the land. You keep the tyres at a low pressure and, if you drive carefully, they leave virtually no marks and can help to flatten out the land.

The quads always make me smile, because they remind me of learning to drive on the farm. Even as a lad, my mode of transport around our fields was a quad. I could disappear off all over the place on the farm with my sheepdog Lace on the back rack and that sense of freedom was incredible for a young lad. I loved just jumping on a quad and zooming around the farm.

In the wintertime when we had snow, we used to fasten a sledge to the back of the quad with a rope and see who could stay on the longest as we went careering round the fields. (We sometimes used skis, after my dad came back from yet another auction with a job lot of them!) We'd be literally full throttle doing circuits of whatever field was available, always in a full-faced helmet because it got really hairy! The only problem was, you'd inevitably get thrown off or crash at some point and end up with all this snow crammed into the space of the helmet where your eyes and nose were exposed. You'd have to dig all this snow out, freezing cold and laughing uncontrollably. Happy days.

I really got into old tractors when I was a young boy. There was a guy down the bottom of the valley called Malcolm who had been around the farm for donkey's years, and he had a yard full of vintage tractors. Me and Malcolm just got on like a house on fire, even though there was probably thirty or so years' age difference between us. He worked in the quarries and on some of the local farms and just had all these amazing stories; I loved listening to him telling them while we were working on the old tractors. I used to go down to his yard and it was like an Aladdin's cave of all this vintage machinery. That place fascinated me.

Malcolm could repair anything; he went everywhere with a tool box of spanners and would repair stuff for locals in the valley. He just wanted to tinker on old machines and help people out. He had a yard with all his kit and these amazing vintage tractors in there, and he used to come up and bring his machines.

He introduced me to this world of vintage tractors and immediately I was totally hooked. The first old tractor I saw him on was a Fordson Major, this beautiful big old blue tractor with red wheels. Fordson Majors were manufactured by Henry Ford & Son Inc. up until 1964 (after which they were all just branded as Ford). Henry Ford himself was brought

up in a large farming family, so he knew what farmers actually needed. To a degree, these tractors were like the Ford Model T of the car world – they were affordable, simple, well designed and reliably built and, most importantly of all for the farming world, they were very versatile and did a brilliant job. The public took to them as soon as they were launched during the First World War, not least because tractors enabled a country at war to produce more food quickly, to feed the nation during the conflict. Ford was not the only manufacturer of tractors, of course, but his machines played a significant part in the mechanization of agriculture. Ford himself once said he wanted 'to lift the burden of farming from flesh and blood and place it on steel and motors' – the first prototype he built in 1907 (using quite a few parts from his cars!) was christened 'an automotive plough'. As the years passed, his tractor brand gained a reputation for being more compact than their competitors and often quite experimental – Malcolm's Ford had a huge drive wheel on the side, which to me as a young lad just looked so cool. You fastened a belt to this drive wheel and then you could attach that to other implements that were separate from the tractor, and use the engine to drive that particular tool. Malcolm had so much stuff: threshers, diggers, dumpers, dozers, every type of machine you could imagine. He also had a Ford 4000 tractor, which he would leave up on the farm; in my mind, that was the ultimate – never mind a Ferrari, give me one of those any day!

Perhaps inevitably, after a while Malcolm started to teach me how to drive. I was so fascinated by all his machines, it was only a matter of time before I asked to drive one of them. I learned to drive on vintage tractors. Sometimes you'd need to use two hands just to get the thing in gear and there was certainly no power-assisted steering or any airbags. The clutches were often pretty brutal, so unless you drove really well, you'd be lurching around the farm like a kangaroo. What those old tractors taught me was to listen to the tone of the engine, work with the sound of the revs, wait for the exact moment to change gear; those old machines really taught me how to drive in tune with each vehicle.

Once I could drive a tractor well, Malcolm started to teach me how to tow trailers. Of course, hardest of all is *reversing* a trailer, but he showed me all the tricks and techniques for that, too. Funnily enough, with my own son Luke, I get him to pull trailers all over the farm, just the same. He can do anything with our 4 × 4 buggy and a flatbed trailer – good lad. I get him to reverse in everywhere, never go in forwards, and he is really good at it now. To this day I have this peculiar pride in my ability to reverse a trailer. It's quite funny, I love turning up somewhere with a cattle trailer and saying, 'Where do you need this?' The harder the reverse, the more I enjoy it.

Around the age of thirteen, I graduated to driving and operating JCBs, too – Malcolm actually lent me a JCB to practise on which, looking back, was very good of him, considering I was only a young teenager! It quickly became the equivalent of a giant games console for me, because you controlled it by two joysticks and all these buttons. So instead of racing cars around a track on a computer, I was lifting piles of stone from one side of our farm track to the other!

I would maintain the track, bringing in the planings – these are the flat, recycled road chippings that we use to keep the potholes under control. I soon moved on to digging out the drains and other useful jobs around the farm.

At the time, I used to do some milking work with a local chap called David Brown. He would pick me up in his Ford Transit and drive us to this dairy farm to work. One day, he parked the van in a field and had to do another job somewhere, so he just gave me the keys and said, 'You go and drive the van over.' I explained I'd only ever driven tractors but he said, 'Haway, man, you'll be fine . . .'

My mum and dad had seen me getting better and better on these various vehicles and started to trust me to operate and drive the few machines we did have on the farm. Any time my parents needed to move a vehicle or machine, it would be, 'Right, Matthew, on you go and shift it, son.'

Of course, with all this experience, by the time I came to trying for my driving test in the first few weeks of 1995, I'd had years of experience. In fact, I only had lessons in a car for a week and then passed first time. The test was only two weeks after my seventeenth birthday, with Christmas in the middle as a total inconvenience! So I just went out on the roads to practise with my mum for seven days beforehand. We would go into town in the Transit van and I would drive around the middle of Durham in the rush hour. Unbelievable!

I was so excited to be out on the road that I swotted up for weeks before the test so that I knew all my theory; I was totally ready to have a go. I took the actual driving test in a Nissan Micra. I will never forget that vehicle: the fans were broken and all the windows were steaming up, so we had to drive along with all of them open – it was bloody freezing. Maybe the guy passed me so he wouldn't have to retest me and risk getting hypothermia.

I loved driving the Transit van after I passed my test. I used to take it to the Durham Sixth Form Centre and sometimes we'd bundle a few friends in. Then we'd get people's orders and go to the McDonald's Drive Thru – we'd pull up at the microphone where they take your order.

'Welcome to McDonald's, how can I help you?'

'Er, can I have twenty Big Mac Meals, please?'

I don't know what it is about driving, but to this day I love it; I find the whole process very relaxing and escapist. I will drive anywhere, in anything, given half the chance. For example, years ago, once it became clear that I would be working in London in TV for the foreseeable future, Nicola and me decided we needed to buy somewhere as a base that was commutable to the TV studios. Of course, we weren't about to buy a flat in the middle of town! So we found a lovely little smallholding in the Chilterns, not dissimilar to the one my parents had up north before they moved to our farm. It meant I could get into town for the TV jobs, but be back home to spend time with our children as they grew up – rather than being away from home several nights a week, which would've been a necessity if I'd based myself at the family farm in Durham. I loved the drive home and the feeling of leaving the fast-paced life behind as I headed for the hills – and likewise I loved the fact that I'd be out with my animals in the morning, then wash the mud off, jump in my Land Rover and head into town for the afternoon, something the *One Show* team often took the mick out of me for.

The place in the Chilterns is also on a hill; we have sheep (Hampshires and Hebrideans), chickens (Silkies and Seramas and laying breeds for eggs), dogs and a cat, so lots of animals. What this means is that my kids have had a pretty much identical life to what I had when I was growing up, a fact that I've worked hard to achieve. We are not dairy farmers, so it is possible to maintain two places like this, you just have to be very organized with well-planned schedules of all the livestock requirements and work. It also helps that the two places are very similar in terms of what is required – the Chilterns smallholding is essentially a small-scale version of what we have in Durham.

As I've said, I love driving so much. Growing up, I always fancied being a lorry driver. I did pass my provisional HGV licence when I was on *Blue Peter* because I wanted to go round personally picking up all the 'Bring and Buy' stuff that viewers were donating for that show's annual *Blue Peter* appeal. I found the low-hanging branches pretty scary, though, you don't realize how low they are until your vehicle's roof is at the same level at 40 mph!

Mum's life could be so much easier if she was as excited by machinery as me, not least after her accident, but mechanizing the farm just isn't going to happen. Tractors and other machinery of that nature just aren't going to work for Mum – on several levels.

Firstly, given the terrain and nature of the soil, which is quite clay-based, it just isn't feasible to crash around in a huge tractor; the massive wheels and weight would just rip up the land. If you hit an incline on a wet day, it would be carnage, those huge wheels would spin and then grip and just churn up the ground.

Secondly, it's not financially viable to buy a £125,000 tractor that you only use a few times each year. So we hire contractors – for example, when it's hay time, we get someone in with all the specialist machinery and they do a fantastic, quick, expert job.

Thirdly – and most importantly for Mum – she just doesn't want loads of modern machinery. She likes traditional methods, she is proud of using them and she enjoys doing so. It's not that she thinks machines don't work, she knows they can be transformational for many farmers, they just aren't her cup of tea. You may have seen an episode of *Our Farm in the Dales* when I surprised her with a tractor I'd borrowed. You can see in her face that she isn't a fan!

It's funny how farm life prepares you for the weirdest moments, so fast-forward from my teenage years learning to drive tractors and JCBs all the way up to 2019, when I found myself in a 'dig-off' with Matt LeBlanc of *Friends* fame, on an episode of *Top Gear*. Matt has a farm of his own – or rather a ranch – out in the States and is also into his tractors, so whenever he'd been on *The One Show*, we did tractor items if we could. We hit it off and would talk a lot about farming, often about the differences in practices here and over there. That's how he came to invite me on to *Top Gear*.

That famous car show filmed a competition to see who could dig the deepest hole in ten minutes with a JCB 3CX back-hoe loader. At the end, they measured each hole to judge the depth . . . and I'd won. It was hilarious and great fun – and I'm pretty sure Malcolm would've been very proud of me!

After the 'dig-off', I did a timed lap of the *Top Gear* track for their 'Star in a Reasonably Priced Car' segment. I did all the test laps with the Stig and that was great fun, but in what was a first in the show's history, they had to cancel my timed lap on the first day's filming as it was too icy and dangerous, meaning I had to go back for a second day to get a timed lap in. On two occasions I actually spun the car fully 360 and, after that, the crew were making comments about me being more like a stunt driver. On the second day, we enjoyed better weather and I clocked in at 1:38.6, putting me in the Top Five on the leader board, behind Chris Hoy (who races cars) and Jay Kay (a big petrolhead).

Sadly, there was no option to race a tractor.

# 9

# Dogs

I've always grown up with dogs, ever since I was young. Mum and Dad have had everything from St Bernards through to giant schnauzers, terriers, collies, everything and anything! Our St Bernard was called Cromwell and he was so big that when I was a child I felt I could almost walk under him. If I close my eyes, I can still feel his jowls wobbling and hear his deep, bellowing bark as I write this. A lovely big bear of a dog, so calm and affectionate: it felt like he would protect me from anything. After Cromwell, we had giant schnauzers: German police dogs, a phenomenal breed. You see quite a few standard and miniature schnauzers but not many giants – obviously they are really big and strong dogs, but also very affectionate and loving.

The first collie that I got for myself was called Lace, who came into my life when I was around eleven years of age (she was called that simply because my mum was going through a period of making lace). Sheepdogs tend to have a one-syllable name so that you are not sending out potentially confusing verbal signals when they are working – they need short snappy names that work alongside the shepherd's commands.

I remember coming home from my first year of comprehensive school all excited, because I knew that Mum had been to get me this puppy. She took me to the stable, I opened the door and looked over the top and there was this dog with huge ears looking up at me and BOOM! . . . instant bond! What a friendship I had with Lace, honestly. I remember sitting in the straw with her straight away and it was one of the best feelings ever. I immediately took her under my wing and we were instantly inseparable.

Even though I was quite young, I desperately

wanted to learn how to work sheepdogs. I'd seen *One Man and His Dog* on the telly and I was obsessed with being able to do what I saw every week on screen – just desperate to have a go – so Mum enrolled me on a course by a sheep-dog handler down in North Yorkshire called Derek Bowmer. Before I started, I took some time to teach Lace a few commands, so that I wasn't starting completely from scratch. I had a high-jump pole in the barn which was part of all of that gym stuff my dad had bought, so I fastened a tennis ball to the end of this pole and I used to swing it round while I was giving her the command for clockwise, 'Come by', or anti-clockwise, 'Away'. Then I would lift the pole in the air and say, 'Lie down'. It was a pretty unconventional way of training a sheepdog but it worked quite well and I got a few of these commands into Lace's head before we started the lessons with Derek.

I turned up on this course and met Derek – he was lovely and had a big white beard, so to my young mind he just looked like Father Christmas. Anyway, there I was, this young lad among older people on the course.

We all showed Derek what our dogs could do. Derek asked could I stop my dog – I could and I showed him. Lace stopped dead in her tracks.

Derek said, 'Right, do you mind if I take her off to the sheep?'

Derek took Lace and off she went with him. I was so proud of her: I remember watching her working with Derek and doing really well – I was *bursting* with pride! After about ten minutes, Derek came back over to me.

'Right,' he said. 'Well, there's two things wrong with this dog.'

I was pretty gutted. Lace seemed to have been doing brilliantly, so I was a little confused by what he'd said.

'Oh, dear, what are they?' I asked, downhearted.

'One: its name.'

'OK...'

'And two: she doesn't belong to me.'

I learned so much from Derek. He's been a great friend over the years and an oracle to help me with my love of sheepdog training.

When your collie is between six months old and a year, you take your dog up to some sheep and you start to see if that 'collie eye' comes in ... the urge to naturally go and run round in circles gathering the sheep. The herding instinct is incredible to witness, that first time you let your pup off with the ewes. It's best to put a long lead or cord on the dog at this age, so that if it gets too excited or carried away, you can control the situation easily. At this point, you basically put them in a small field and help them naturally discover their instinct, hopefully circling the sheep, but then you start to work with that instinctive, natural behaviour by adding in commands. Through loads of repetitions, the dog begins to associate the commands with what it is doing at that moment. Over time, the dog becomes completely used to the commands and once that happens, you're in business.

The basic commands are typically two syllables, so as well as the ones I taught Lace first ('Come by' for clockwise, 'Away' for anti-clockwise), there is also 'Get on', when you want your dog to move forward and push on, while 'Lie down' is the other, slightly more self-explanatory command. You also use 'Look back', to spin your dog on its haunches and go back in the direction that it came from, to pick up any sheep they may have left behind them. And finally you have 'That'll do' for when you are saying, 'Game over, let's leave the field.'

When you are actually herding the sheep with a trained, experienced dog, the first thing you ask of your dog is to run all the way around the outside of the field – known as 'the outrun' – hopefully making sure that every single sheep or lamb is collected up on the way past. Once they are in the middle, you would shout 'Lie down!' when your dog's in a twelve o'clock position in relation to you . . . and this is the absolutely amazing part when instinct cuts in . . . the dog will naturally want to bring the sheep to you. It is just magical to be a part of. You use the command 'Get on' or 'Walk up', which will take the dog closer to the sheep.

If, say, the dog has brought the sheep halfway up the field and suddenly sees a sheep has popped out of a gorse bush or whatever at the top of the field that they've missed, that's when you say 'Look back' and it will spin round and run all the way back to go and collect the loose sheep.

If it looks like the sheep are starting to run or chase, then you would lie your dog down again and then get it to gently come forward by saying, 'Get on, get on.' If some sheep drift to one side or the other, you then use your 'Come by' or 'Away' commands to correct that left or right, just gradually working the sheep to where you want them. What you are aiming for is a situation called 'the perfect balance', which basically means that the sheep and dog are running at a nice tempo, they are not freaked out or frightened, they're just moving at a very positive, measured speed.

This is obviously simplifying the unbelievable craft of shepherding to just a few paragraphs – I could write an entire book about the subject! There're all sorts of topics, such as shedding, penning, driving and many more . . . but hopefully this gives you an idea of the skill, craft and relationship between us and our dogs.

Me and Lace were as thick as thieves, best pals; we always had such a brilliant time on the hills. In fact, at first she was less than impressed with Nicola's presence there, because Lace wanted me all to herself. So if we were going on the quad, Lace would leg it really fast and jump up on there, then sit as close to me as possible so that Nicola couldn't get in between us! The looks that she used to throw at Nicola were really quite something. But over time, she accepted and bonded with Nicola and before long the three of us would be off all over the farm together.

She taught me so much, did Lace, she was fantastic. We would also drive around in that Transit van and she would put her paws up on the back of the seat, with her big ears sticking up. I'd be driving along talking to her and whenever I looked in the rear-view mirror, she'd be there, like my own black-and-white Batman in the back, looking out over the world.

What a beautiful dog. I was devastated when she passed away. All our dogs are buried on the farm. They are all looking over the same view in the front field. That's as it should be.

*

After I started on *Blue Peter*, if you recall, I moved away from the city to a cottage with a paddock an hour or so outside of London, just to find some nature and be around countryside. Then I got the sheep that I mentioned and so, obviously, I needed a sheepdog! That's when I got Meg, who *Blue Peter* viewers may well remember.

Derek Bowmer, the sheepdog trainer who had taught me so much and who'd loved Lace, then found Meg for us; he said she was the perfect one and he was right – she was incredible. Derek knew of a neighbouring farm in the Dales, not too far away, where the lady had a litter of sheepdog puppies. We actually went and filmed the whole story with *Blue Peter*. I remember going along there and seeing Meg for the first time; she was absolutely beautiful as a little puppy – beforehand, I'd had in my mind what I wanted in terms of really traditional collie markings and she fitted the bill perfectly. The second I saw her, I knew that she was the one for me. We had to go back a few times until she was old enough to bring home, then finally it was time to film the collection. I put Meg on a towel on my lap and she came on the long trip down south. When we got home, I put her on the mat by the door while I went to unpack the car, and Nicola tells the story of how she looked at Meg, then Meg looked at her as if to say, 'Right, well, what happens next?'

Meg obviously wasn't related to Lace, but she also had pricked-up ears – it's like some sort of weird Baker-family-dog trait! Meg settled quickly into life on the smallholding down south and immediately started coming into London with me to work on *Blue Peter*, including in the actual studio. To be honest with you, at times it was an absolute nightmare having a working collie in a television studio! For me, as somebody who loves the concept of dog training, it was too much. What you didn't see behind the cameras was the basketball team warming up, the studio doors opening, double-decker buses coming in and out, the pop bands in and the music going, so both Meg and me had our work cut out! It's challenging enough doing a live TV show, but doing that while keeping an eye out for a working sheepdog was pretty tiring some days! If you think about it, the environment she was in for *Blue Peter* couldn't have been more alien to her natural habitat on our farm, yet she took it all in her stride; she was just amazing.

Meg was so clever. As the music started for the *Blue Peter* theme tune, she somehow seemed to know that my attention needed to be elsewhere. But she could be a little cheeky: she'd often be off running round the studio, rounding up and herding the entire crew! At one point, the pop band S Club 7 were on the show and as their performance was being introduced, I thought, *Where the hell is Meg?* I looked at the monitor and there she was, with her paws on the singer Tina's back end, walking through the shot while they were all singing! It was absolutely hilarious!

When Meg was under command, I could get her to do anything. She was a real action dog, so we did all sorts of stories on the show with other working dogs – sniffer dogs, police dogs and military dogs. Meg went through the training as well, so she was pretty multi-skilled in the end.

Meg had a little red collar that was her kind of 'show' outfit, but actually she loved nothing more than just being muddy when we got back to my little cottage with the paddock; it was great for her to blow off steam and do her thing and be a proper sheepdog after working in a TV studio all day.

I guess for a time Meg was the most famous dog in the country, being on that show. Our viewers took her to their hearts. I soon realized that a lot of those children who watched *Blue Peter* didn't have the opportunity to own a dog themselves, so when they saw Meg on the telly, and watched her grow up and eventually have puppies of her own, they felt she was part of their family. Incidentally, Meg's puppies went off to become mountain rescue and hearing dogs, and we followed those stories on the show as well, which was just perfect.

We lost Meg not long after our first child, Luke, was born. Sometimes we would be looking for her, wondering where she had got to, and we'd find her lying under Luke's cot as he slept; she used to want to look after him, making sure he was OK. When we lost her shortly after, it was heart-breaking, especially after everything we had been through and experienced together. Meg was the ultimate connection between my work and everything I had learned at home on the farm; she had seen me develop through my *Blue Peter* career and had always been there by my side, right up to seeing us welcome our first child.

After a life of having dogs around me all the time, I was very keen to do the same for my own children. When the kids were really young, we got a black Lab called Annie, because I wanted a dog that was going to be 'bomb proof' from a child's perspective, just a calm dog that they'd be able to grab and run and jump on its back and all that kind of stuff. She was brilliant with them back then, just a dream dog for children that age. She is getting old now, but she's still a mellow, calming, beautiful personality.

At the time of writing, we have just had a litter

of cairn terriers: beautiful little dogs, and so full of energy. It was quite a handful for Mum, having just had her accident, but she loves rearing pups. In terms of the farm life, we also have another working collie; he is called Bob. He is a beautiful boy, really lovely, and has been fantastic for my children, too. He is running on 100 per cent pure instinct though, all the time. Annie will amble over and play, but Bob will sit, literally ALL DAY, with his nose pointing at the sheep through the fence. He just stares at them for HOURS, never moving. When you actually let him work with the sheep . . . wow . . . Heavens, then he is the happiest dog in the world. Annie will go out for a wee and then be straight back in front of the fire or sniffing around the oven, whereas Bob . . . you could go shopping, I could go and present *The One Show* and come back again, and Bob would still be by the fence, lying there, looking at the sheep, thinking, *This is the best view ever!* Funnily enough, if you take Bob somewhere in the house where he can't see the sheep, he suddenly becomes like a lap dog, so he has got two modes. I have never experienced a collie like him; he's a real dude. He is also really photogenic – when we filmed him for *Our Farm in the Dales,* he was like a movie star, being filmed in slow-motion with his coat wafting majestically in the wind, like a mane on some black-and-white lion of the valley.

One wonderful perk of my job is that I commentate on *One Man and His Dog*, which has been taken under the umbrella of *Countryfile*. That is always a highlight of every series for me! We have teams from each nation, as well as young handlers, it's fantastic to be involved in and I love that we are giving a platform to such a traditional skill. For me personally, being involved in *One Man and His Dog* also gives me a wonderful sense of coming full circle from my days as a young lad watching that programme every week and desperately wanting to be able to do what those farmers and shepherds were doing on telly.

My love of the art of sheepdog trialling and training is something that has always stayed with me. It's an unbelievable art form and I'd actually like to go back to trialling, to spend more time working on the competitive side of that skill. I keep going back to that feeling of balance when you live and work on a farm, and seeing a sheepdog at work, instinctively herding the sheep, just gives me a huge sense of place every time.

And that's dogs in a nutshell. You can have the worst of days and yet when you come back home, they will be so happy to see you: no grudges, no arguments, no awkwardness, it's so pure. The only thing they want is to be with you and there is no better feeling.

A wagging tail is such a great healer.

Ultimately, the reason why we love animals so much is because the only time they break hearts is when they leave us.

## IO

# In Tune with Nature

My passion for being in tune with nature isn't just for me in the Durham hills. It is universal and it's global. One of the greatest privileges that was gifted to me when working on *Blue Peter* was the unbelievable overseas expeditions we were sent on, out in the wild all over the world. There are so many incredible memories from my travels with that show, but in the context of this idea of being around nature, there is one trip to Morocco that I have very special memories from. We went to the Atlas Mountains and I lived for three days with a nomad called Ali Louche, who was seventy-three years old and had thirteen kids! We didn't speak a word of each other's language, but somehow he knew I was into the same way of life that he was – maybe by the way I was around his goats, helping him to move them about, maybe by the way I reacted to the environment. Who knows the exact reasons – there was just this unspoken understanding between us. To be there in the mountains and to feel nature in that way, to be sleeping out under the stars where you could see the curvature of the earth, just lying there, I was in my element. Ali Louche cooked these incredible goat kebabs on his fire in front of me and we made some bread. It was magical. We had so much in common, we would sit there waving our hands around, some- how communicating easily.

Incredibly, Ali Louche had not travelled very far at all in his own life, in fact he had never been on the other side of his mountain before. Somehow, we stayed in touch and he made it known that he wanted to come and see how I lived. We put him on an aero- plane – can you imagine? His brain must have been flipping – and he came to stay at our farm. When he first arrived at the airport, I took him in a lift to get to my car but he couldn't work out why the scenery was changing every time the doors opened – simply because he hadn't realized he was going up.

We set up a bedroom for him but he wouldn't go in there, he wanted to sleep by the fire, down in the lounge. He also wanted to kill our lambs and eat them for dinner, because that was the only way he knew how to feed his family. He even offered to slaughter one of the lambs for tea, so I had to explain that that wasn't the plan! He wandered around the farm with his traditional clothing on; it was just a brilliant sight to see. One afternoon we took him to the coast because he had never seen the sea before, and he was kneeling down in the water, just crying and praying. At that exact moment, a rainbow appeared, and I was like . . . *This is unbelievable.* To watch someone at the age of seventy-three witnessing all these things (that we take for granted) for the first time ever was quite incredible.

This mutual love of the countryside and common ground that farming people share was apparent many times during all my travels. You might think that being out here, a thousand feet above sea level in the Durham hills, means we have a very specific style of farming, peculiar to the local area and climate. In many ways, that would be the case, yes; however, I have been lucky enough to witness first-hand the different types of farming and countryside-living around the globe and it is clear that there is a universality to this way of life – there might be thousands of miles distance between two farmers, but they will always find something in common.

Another example of this was when I travelled to Vietnam. We visited a 'floating community' that farmed fish under their huts; it was just incredible to see them at work and play. They had been living like this for centuries, in all these different sizes and styles of 'buildings' on rafts on the water. In the morning, the children would all paddle out across the water to a floating schoolroom. Then the adults would go out in these hand-made coracles, fishing for hours, dragging nets behind them, then they would bring their catch back home to their hut, lift up the floorboards, and empty the net into the space underneath where their home floated. As a general rule, the biggest fish were traded, and the smaller ones went under the hut. Any food waste was also used naturally – up went the floorboards again and the leftover scraps became fish food. And the genius part was, these smaller fish would quickly grow to be bigger fish – not least because they were in a safe, predator-free environment under these huts – and at some point they would be big enough to trade. Talk about totally making the best of your circumstances.

I never cease to be amazed at how the world feeds itself.

You might wonder where the commonality with our farm in the Dales lies . . . well, like them, we are always looking at ways to blend seamlessly into our environment; we look to make as little negative impact as practically possible and, always, we aim to live from one season to the next, enjoying whatever that time of year brings to its fullest.

My TV career has gifted me so many opportunities to be around, and in tune with, nature, and I am very grateful for that. I was lucky enough to be part of a wildlife programme called *Big Blue Live* which was filmed in Monterey Bay; it was ground-breaking telly at the time actually, as we managed to get the first blue whale ever filmed on live TV. I took Mum on that trip, because I just knew this was going to be a once-in-a-lifetime opportunity for her to go and sit and watch the whales, so she, Nicola and my children came out with me. Gosh, to be in the presence of those huge animals and see them breaching and swimming wild in the water, wow . . .

I was similarly in awe when I went to the habitat of Kodiaks, the world's biggest brown bears. Crikey, they are BIG. We stayed in this shack on Kodiak island in Alaska. One morning, we trekked quite some way to this river and found these massive bears fishing in the shallows. When they heard us, they turned to look and then they just went back to their task, because thankfully it was the salmon run, so we knew that those bears would be more interested in the fish than us!

Likewise, being lucky enough to see wild cheetahs in Tanzania just reminded me again how powerful and graceful wildlife can be. Also, when I was sleeping out in the Serengeti and hearing lions padding around our tent at night . . . I couldn't help thinking, *I am actually a potential part of their food chain right now!* Jokes aside, it did make me think, *These animals are all out there, every day and night, fighting to survive.* That idea that *you could simply be a meal* is a really sobering thought. When I go on trips like that, it always gives me a stark reminder of the power of nature.

Of course, this universality of loving Mother Nature and the world around us isn't confined just to farmers and those who work in the countryside or travel the world. During my time on *The One Show*, I was constantly amazed at how many very high-profile guests came on the show and wanted to talk to me about their passion for nature. This wouldn't always be on camera, because often they'd necessarily be promoting a film or book or similar. However, in between VTs, I often found myself striking up conversations with the most incredibly diverse range of people who all had one thing in common: a love of nature. For example, Paul O'Grady lives and loves that life, he is such a passionate champion of animals; Lord Andrew Lloyd Webber is a farmer; the Who's lead singer, Roger Daltrey, is also really enthusiastic about farming. A lot of these stars knew I was on *Countryfile*, so that would often be the trigger for us to start talking. You'd be amazed who I have ended up talking about tups and lambing with!

As a quick aside, while I am on the subject of country music, for my dad's seventieth birthday, I surprised him with tickets to Nashville, which had long been a dream of his. He doesn't travel very well these days and I knew that he would have got himself all worked up if he had known the trip was coming, so instead we took him out for a surprise birthday lunch. Then, while we were all sitting at the table, I pulled out some plane tickets to Nashville for us both!

'What?! When are we going, son?'

'Right now, Dad . . . Mum's packed your suitcase already!'

We had the most amazing trip. I had phoned a really brilliant music producer called Mark Hagen who worked for Radio 2 and he'd made some calls on our behalf and arranged the most amazing access to recording studios, all sorts, when we got to

Nashville – we got behind the scenes everywhere! Great memories.

People who love nature in terms of seasonality have a common ground, too. Just a way of life in the countryside where you make the most of every opportunity that each month brings. That's why it makes very little sense to me to go to all the trouble of selling out-of-season fruit or vegetables when each of the four seasons of our year provide the most wonderful variety and supply of seasonal produce.

In the springtime, I am a massive fan of pickled beetroot, but I am also very partial to a rhubarb crumble around that time. I love spring onions in a salad in March, with some salad cream and iceberg lettuce, and maybe a few soft new potatoes. Summer radishes are a delight, and who doesn't crave a few punnets of strawberries in the hotter months? I don't think there is a better taste than eating peas straight out of the pod. I love sweet peas. Also in the summer, my mum used to cook a whole cauliflower and put it in the middle of the table with melted cheddar all over it – sometimes it looked like some kind of cheesy brain! In the autumn, you have carrots, the earliest parsnips, too – oh man, roasted parsnips are without doubt my favourite vegetable, I would say.

I love eating tomatoes straight off the vine around summer/autumn, too. Winter veg like sprouting broccoli is splendid. I think maybe cabbage is my favourite seasonal veg, but there's so much choice . . .

OK, I need to stop now, because my mouth is actually watering thinking about all this seasonal fruit and veg . . .

The point I am trying to make is that you have so much variety, so much taste, colour, so many beautiful aromas if you just eat with the seasons, you will never be short of the most wonderful food.

Apart from the taste, which in my opinion is always far greater in seasonal produce, if you eat this way you are also living in tune with our year. You are working alongside nature, not against it. That is an entirely authentic, symbiotic relationship, where you are utilizing what is naturally available, which in many ways has been lost in the constant modern craving for any type of food at any time of the year. Maybe I am too sensitive to this subject, being so close to the heart of the matter, but for example, I heard some-one on the radio talking about eating strawberries in the middle of winter and I just thought, *What a shame*. It certainly isn't down to a lack of choice! We have become so used to having what we want, when we want it, that it never feels special; whereas I cele-brate seasonal veg, I really do. I don't wear jumpers in the summer, and I don't wear shorts in the winter, so why do that with your food?

When me and Nicola got married, we could think of nowhere better to celebrate than on the farm, making the most of our surroundings. We got married in 2004 in a local church, way up on the top of a hill. There was a sign attached to the gate with baler twine that said, 'Sheep in churchyard'. We had a reception in a local country hotel then all went back to the farm and had a weekend of celebration. Everyone was camping in the front field, which wasn't ideal for those guests who had too much to drink and ended up rolling down the hill in their tent! We did our very own Highland Games, where we had a full schedule of 'bride's family versus groom's' events. We did tug o' war, inflatable footballs, clay pigeon shoot, rounders, loads of food, tents filled with punch and beer, wines. We had a karaoke and a disco, we sat around a fire playing drums, and in the courtyard we had a local folk band performing traditional music; they had squeeze boxes, guitars and mouth organs, and we all learned the dances, skipping and jumping round the courtyard; it was everything we'd dreamed of. By the end of the weekend, people were strewn everywhere, sleeping in barns, tents – we had such a great time! It was just so wonderful for me and Nicola to start our married life together in that way.

In terms of being in tune with your surroundings, one of the most intense experiences I ever had – and also one of the scariest – was being up in the clouds when I broke a world record for tandem hang-gliding. I might suggest that if you ever want to learn about clouds, there might be easier and less anxious ways of doing it, but you know me, I tend to throw myself into things full on!

The idea was to attempt the record for the highest-ever tandem hang-glider flight, all filmed for *Blue Peter*, of course. I was paired with this fabulous husband and wife team, Judy Leden (one of the world's top hang-gliding pilots) and her elite trainer husband, Chris Dawes. Chris was the man to tutor me and Judy had the unenviable task of going up into the sky with an inexperienced Durham farmer!

Obviously, I had to learn how to fly a hang-glider myself, otherwise I would've just been a deadweight for Judy. It was a long old process of turning up on this airfield, training, going up with Judy, then aiming to eventually go up solo before attempting the world record with her. When you start, it is quite manageable: you are towed by a winch system to a certain height, just like a big kite really, and then you disconnect the cable and you are up there, no engine obviously, just flying like a bird. Gosh, what a feeling to be up there so high without a motor. There's this sense that you are in a place that you shouldn't be; it's a weird feeling because you are in a completely alien environment. It's so calm and quiet, serene, almost surreal. With no engine to control, you have to use your body to manoeuvre the hang-glider, so you push the bar in front of you away and it will stall the glider, then you pull it back and the glider will stabilize; it is really subtle. The 'best of the best' hang-gliders are so skilled and watching Judy was just so impressive.

Eventually, it came to the day where I had to go up solo for the first time. The idea was for me to get winched up into the sky about five hundred feet, circle around in certain safe patterns for a while, then make my way back down to earth.

On that first solo flight, that wasn't exactly what happened.

I went up like this big kite – so far so good. I picked up the wind and was cruising steadily, I felt good, I felt safe, I felt – relatively – in control. I was supposed to do one full circle then land safely.

When, suddenly, I got caught in a rapid rising thermal . . .

And where does hot air go?

Up.

And up.

And up.

In what felt like a few seconds, I had rocketed way higher than I was expecting and, worse still, I was rapidly drifting a long way from the airfield. Nicola and my dad were down below, and she said afterwards that it was pretty terrifying, watching me disappear into the clouds, a long way from them, without knowing how I was doing.

By this point, all thoughts of doing a nice, neat circle as planned and then landing had gone out of the window. I was just concentrating on not having a very serious incident. I love watching the clouds and being up close with them, but not that close! I was in self-preservation mode and really having to concentrate not to panic or do the wrong thing. I was looking at my altitude meter and the number was getting larger and larger . . . suddenly I was at a thousand feet . . .

Somehow, I managed to turn and head back in the general direction of the airfield, although it was becoming clear that I wasn't going to actually land in the safest of ways. I knew there was a good chance that I wouldn't even make it to the airfield to land at all.

Back on the ground, Nicola and Dad were obviously panicked, but Chris was brilliant, he was reassuring them that I had done all the correct training and that I knew what to do to stay safe. We had a two-way radio and he was talking to me, advising and keeping me calm, but at one point, the radio crackled and fell silent – I can tell you, it wasn't very enjoyable for those few seconds being that high without any communication with the ground!

Luckily, the radio sparked back into life and, with Chris's expert help, I was able to guide the hang-glider down to a more manageable height. All I had to do now was land. The funny part – although I don't remember laughing at the time – was that as I came in to land, I could see a big main road and I was heading straight for it! I guided my glider just high enough to avoid the road, but on the *Blue Peter* footage from the various cameras that we'd set up on the glider itself, you can see me coming in pretty fast with all these lorries zooming past, not that far below me.

Anyway, I somehow made it over the road and over the airfield fence and finally came in to land . . .

In a tree.

That was not the landing I was expecting for my very first solo flight, but at least I was down in one piece!

At the end of the day, when you are up in the clouds, you may be the world's most experienced hang-glider but you will never be as powerful as Mother Nature. That's why the top hang-gliders are always reverential towards and respectful of their environment. For example, there is a phenomenon known as 'cloud suck' where pilots experience a sharp and significant lift due to thermals under cumulus clouds, and it is possibly this which caused me to catapult straight up into the heavens. Hang-gliders become experts at reading a cloud shape; they sense the atmosphere and are able to gauge the likely weather behaviour . . . it is all incredibly nuanced and skilful.

That experience just shows you how powerful nature is. I had done all the training, Chris and Judy had done an amazing job, but that sudden thermal just took the situation out of my hands. You always have to respect nature; once you start to dismiss its power and scale, you are in trouble, especially if that happens when you are thousands of feet in the air underneath a big kite.

We were really unlucky with unsuitable weather; we practised for ages but had so many days called off. Obviously, you just can't risk a flight if the weather isn't ideal; there is too much potential danger. It was one of those projects that just kept getting cancelled and pushed back and pushed back and pushed back. I continued my training and eventually the big day arrived when the weather was right and we could go for the world record. I woke up one morning, opened the curtains and looked out of the window – clear blue sky – and I just knew the weather was in our favour . . . that was such an exciting moment, mixed with real trepidation.

I had to wear this unbelievable outfit, which was like a massive sleeping bag: an all-in-one mountaineering suit for really low temperatures at high altitude, complete with these enormous snow boots. I kissed Nicola and Dad goodbye, then before I knew it, me and Judy were up in the clouds being towed by Chris in his microlight.

It is weird when you are filming these mad stunts and crazy experiences, you almost forget that it's real life, you are sort of focused on making the story and you always feel you are going to be OK, but at the same time, this was genuinely potentially dangerous. Of course, Judy was in complete control. We kept getting higher and higher and then I realized that the height had stopped being a factor, because everything down on the ground had become so small that I couldn't tell the difference between two points, we'd got so high.

We continued our ascent, up through the cloud base, and then we were able to look *down* on the clouds – that was an amazing moment. WOW!

The clouds almost looked as though they were the

ground, if that doesn't sound too crazy. I obviously couldn't see the actual ground by this point, so being above the clouds meant they were my only reference point below. It was so surreal and so spectacular. We were just in this otherworldly zone, this vast expanse of sky and cloud . . . unbelievable. It was like a dream. All I could hear was the wind rushing into my full-faced helmet; we were, quite literally, flying.

I am very proud to say that me and Judy broke the world record, hitting an astonishing altitude of 11,000 feet. That's two miles up in the sky!

As utterly wonderful as that record-breaking experience was, I have never felt the need to do any more hang gliding since. I have kind of parked that, left that there, up in those clouds. I prefer to look at the clouds from down below.

Having trekked around the globe making TV features about so many different countryside folk, I feel incredibly blessed that just after my mum's accident, I actually got the opportunity to make a show much closer to home – in fact, set in my home!

After leaving *The One Show* in the spring of 2020, I had started my own production company – Big Circus Media – with the intention of making high-end documentaries and factual entertainment shows. Ever since I first started in television, I had been fascinated by the process of making programmes. Even back then, as a twenty-year-old lad, I used to go and sit in the edit with the directors and the editors on an evening after a long day's filming, just to see how they created these shows from the footage that I'd been involved with. I would sit there for hours, soaking it all in like a sponge.

So television production is something I've always loved getting heavily involved with. Every show that I've done, I loved the process of deciding what we are going to cover and why, working out the best way to approach our subjects to get the best results. This was the best bit of *The One Show* for me – as the show was going out, the last thing I was thinking about was me; instead, I was most focused on what our viewers were experiencing, and what did we need more or less of, as the case may be.

I have had a long-term passion for *making* TV programmes, not just *presenting* them. I love to really get to grips with the subject and be as big a part as I can in terms of the way that each story is put across to the viewers. I'm not the kind of person that just turns up and delivers some lines and walks away again, I just get too immersed in what I'm doing.

I was very sad to leave *The One Show*. People would often say to me, 'Oh, don't you get bored doing it every weekday?' but I never did; every single show was different and I was fortunate to meet some of the most remarkable guests. I also made many fantastic friends during my time there, including becoming very close pals with Alex Jones (it was actually me who presented with her for her audition!). However, with my longstanding fascination with the production side of the process, when I left that programme, my absolute priority was to start up my own production company – finally. I did so with my great friend Gareth Collett, who I'd first met when I joined *The One Show* – at the time he was the series producer, later going on to be Head of Development for BBC Studios.

Now, when Mum had her accident, I had to work from up on the farm while I helped her recover and get the farm under control. Along the way, Gareth and I were having various video calls, conversations with TV commissioners about potential new shows and, of course, the chats would sometimes get around to where I was and what I was doing.

We were having one of these chats with a great guy from More4 called Sean Doyle, and he was asking me questions about the farm and listening intently when I told him all the changes we were already making. I was chattering away, just explaining about fairly random stuff like moving the chickens, making better shelter for the sheep in winter, just nattering really . . .

He said, 'Matt, would you film it? And make a TV show about what's happening?'

It was never my intention to film the farm or my family: we were just there to help Mum out of her difficult situation. Putting this on TV was not on my radar. To be honest, I was more focused on working on TV ideas that didn't involve me, let alone my family!

I had previously been asked to film a series on the farm, but I'd never wanted to, as I wanted total control over it. I wanted to direct, produce and present it and that would not have been possible without my own production company. I spoke to Nicola, my parents and the children and there was a general feeling that it could be quite fun. So I worked up a concept on the kitchen table, took some photos around the farm and created a presentation on my laptop of the vision and perspective that I wanted to take: the angle of helping my parents to continue doing what they love and changing the farm to allow that to happen. The plan was for the show to be authentic and, above all, relatable to people who didn't live in the countryside.

I rang a cameraman friend of mine who I'd done a lot of lockdown filming for *Countryfile* with. I also rang another friend, a sound man from Cumbria who I met on my second-ever foreign filming trip twenty-odd years ago. Mum, Dad and Nicola knew him well, as we'd done loads of filming on the farm together over the years. Gareth got everything sorted at the other end and got an editor confirmed . . . and it was that simple.

My children were at an age when they could make up their own minds. Part of my reason for not featuring them before now was that I've always wanted to wait to give them the choice about whether they felt comfortable being involved in what I did for a living, so we fully included them in the decision and they were, of course, totally free to say they didn't want us to do it.

Initially, I said that we would film a pilot and if the family decided they weren't comfortable with it, we would simply not do anything with the footage. It all happened in real time – we filmed Mum going, for the first time, back to the sheep pen where she had been knocked over, we painted the donkey stables, filmed a bit with the chickens.

As soon as I got the footage in the edit, I knew it was going to work.

As promised to my family and myself, I was across every second of footage and crafted it in a way that we were all happy with. Gareth was totally on board with this and offered me incredible support and understanding, and tried to make the whole process as smooth as possible.

I was proud of what we'd created and, to be honest, it didn't matter how the show performed in terms of ratings, because it was authentic and it was how I see my family in the place I grew up.

I showed my family the edit.

'What do you think?' I asked everyone.

'It's all right, isn't it?' said Mum, smiling.

Then, not for the first time in my life, my parents said, 'Matthew . . . go for it!'

And that is how *Our Farm in the Dales* was born.


We had a rule that if anyone didn't like any part of any of the footage, then we would not use it. In fact, much of the footage from that pilot made the first episode. Sean at More4 was very supportive and so, in March 2021, the first episode was screened, exactly a year to the day after I left *The One Show*. The night of the debut was really nerve-racking. We all huddled up in the courtyard and I rigged up this projector that shone the show on to one of the courtyard walls. It was a strange feeling – this was my home, my family, my directing and executive-producing debut, as well as my production company's first-ever show.

The whole thing had taken over my life for six months – the planning, the directing, the editing, the process of delivering a series and being across every inch was so incredibly intense, not to mention the fact it was with my family and we'd re-versioned the whole farm in the process. It was madness.

We'd all worked so hard and got to the end of this crazy time together, and just to sit there and watch the fruits of our labours – together, actually there with everyone – was wonderfully bizarre. And really special.

You simply don't know how the viewing public are going to react. An England football match had been on the same evening, and there was a worry about competing with that, so we were all shocked and delighted to find that the programme had smashed More4's record for best viewing figures ever! Over 1.15 million people had tuned in that night and totalled over 1.8 million a few days later!

At its heart, what we filmed is a *family*; yes, of course, that's set against the backdrop of the farm, but the show is about those family decisions that we all have to make in our lives when the tables turn and you start to take care of your parents in the way that they have done for you. This was a time when the whole family stepped up. That is the heartbeat of the show and thankfully it seemed to resonate with people. I do wonder if the lockdown we were all in at the time reminded people of the importance of family and perhaps that struck a chord with some viewers, too. I also think the simplicity and escapism of our farm seems to appeal, just letting the viewers watch us, as a family, navigate our way through a challenging time and pull together to make life better for everyone. Also, it was an example of the kind of programmes I love to make, which have something for all ages to enjoy; the engagement comes from heart, not from any jeopardy.

I've always tried to make TV that is genuine; as viewers, we all know when something is manufactured, and I think if you treat the audience with respect and make honest shows, they reward you with their support.

On the point of authenticity in TV, let me digress for a moment and tell you about a filming experience I had that really taught me a very important lesson in always being honest with the programmes you make. I went to the Olympic diving centre to film a piece about that very impressive sport. Firstly, I interviewed a very talented young diver and – in a nod to my original *Blue Peter* audition – they asked me to do that while we were both bouncing up and down on a trampoline! Then, at the end of the day's shoot, the plan was to film me diving off the high diving board, some ten metres up. I started by diving off the three-metre board, then the five-, then the seven-and-a-half-metre one (which felt VERY high), but when I got to the ten-metre board, I FROZE.

I couldn't bring myself to do it.

Even with all my gymnastics experience, where you can find yourself in very precarious physical situations, I found this was another level in terms of fear and perceived danger. It was going against all your natural instincts.

I stood there for what felt like an age.

Eventually, I said, 'Can I just jump off feet first?'

The diving coach said if I did that, it would be harder to convince myself to go head first.

To make matters worse, there was a problem with the jets by the pool – they use these to spray the top of the water, so that you can see the surface that you are aiming for and gauge the distance. Without these jets, all I could see was the bottom of the pool, which looked like a postage stamp!

Remember, I had done loads of dangerous and risky things for *Blue Peter*: I'd been filmed hanging off cliffs, I had done cable-car rescues over ravines, deep-sea diving, I'd been filmed with the marines, with paratroopers, rock-climbed the Todgha Gorge in Morocco, among many other adventures. However, on that day, perched on that high diving board, I just felt so scared – standing there in just a pair of swimming trunks looking down at a tiny pool of water that looked a mile away.

I felt stuck.

I'm not gung-ho. I'm not one of these adrenaline junkies that does something because they're up for a challenge, I'm not that.

By this point, I was getting frustrated with myself, at the situation, at the fact we needed to get the film done. Then the cameraman at the poolside shouted up and said, 'Matt, really sorry, mate, but I'm going to have to go now . . . I've been here for ages, seriously, we're going to have to leave . . .'

I needed that line to be drawn, that ultimatum.

I dived.

I'll never forget the time it took to hit the water . . . it felt like an ETERNITY . . . the wind rushing past my ears, the constant reassessment of my body shape through the air . . .

I eventually hit the water.

In the calmness of the underwater world that followed, I remember feeling so relieved. I stayed in this
slow-motion state for as long as my breath allowed,
knowing I'd conquered a real challenge. Then I swam
to the side of the pool and said to the cameraman,
'I'm never going to do that again!'

The point I wanted to make is that the audience
reaction to that piece was the most overwhelming
of anything I'd filmed at that time. The producers
of *Blue Peter* left my anxieties and hesitation in the
edit for all to see, and people really empathized and
warmed to the fact we weren't pretending I just
calmly and heroically climbed up there and dived
off. The letters that I got from children who were
going through difficult times were just so enlighten-
ing to me as a film-maker. They were saying the film
had helped them face their fears, and given them
strength. I felt so touched that my own struggle and
honesty on that diving board had helped so many
viewers.

And that taught me about honesty in filming. The
response wasn't about the diving itself, although
that was interesting enough – these children weren't
writing about wanting to become divers; they were
writing to say they had felt encouraged to face their
fears and push through. They liked that I was obviously, visibly petrified but still went ahead and did

it. I felt very honoured that the piece garnered that reaction and I learned a very valuable lesson in TV in the process. So, hopefully, with *Our Farm in the Dales*, viewers felt we applied the same authenticity, the same truthfulness.

Moving forward into the future, I will never stop presenting; I love that side of it but I'm really enjoying coming up with different programme ideas and offering my input not just from a presenter's perspective now, but also from what I've learned through the years of so many different styles of television programmes.

From a personal point of view, apart from being very proud of my family, who did an amazing job in a completely new venture for them, I really enjoyed the process of just being spontaneous, unscripted, just going with whatever happened and what was said was what you saw. Having spent many years in *The One Show* production office, making our TV show about the farm felt very liberating, not least in terms of my dyslexia.

It is strange how I've ended up in a career that revolves around scripts. You can imagine how daunting reading an autocue can be for someone in my situation. If anybody hands me scripts or anything written down, I look at them but I can't read them. It's weird. Like I say, over the years I appear to have developed a photographic memory, so once I have seen something I can recall it completely. When I do any pieces to camera, I will look at the script and see it in my mind's eye, then I will recite what I have memorized. I can almost picture it – I don't *learn* lines; I *look* at lines and I see them in my mind. Producers will fire off a script and send it to me as if that's job done, whereas for me that is only the beginning of the challenge. Translating those words into good television is the tricky part. I have learned to judge what people are trying to get at, then I will say it in my own way . . . that's the only way to do it, for me.

That's why the most frightening thing that can happen to me on live television is suddenly being handed a piece of paper with an email, and being asked to read that out. To read something out cold is really quite difficult for me.

I use a special type of font on my computer; its design is weighted in a certain way so that the letters are heavier at the bottom than they are at the top, and, for me, this helped stop some of the words from jumping around. (We put it on the autocue so I could use it during the show.)

What I will say is that I feel my dyslexia has inadvertently gifted me with an interview style that people seem to find relaxing. I can't rattle off every word on an autocue or script, almost without thinking, it's just not possible. However, I don't want to – I want to have an informal chat with the guests. I'd like to think this more casual approach puts contributors at ease when they realize that they are just having a conversation with someone who happens to be on TV. I actually dislike the term 'interview', because to me it never is an interview, it is just a chat. I am so intrigued by folk and by the subjects that they have dedicated their lives to, so that is always my technique, to simply have a chat about what makes them tick. The fact that my dyslexia fuels this means I have developed a style over the years of interpreting the research and script in my own way.

Although I am very at home with presenting a live TV show, I don't think I will ever find reading aloud relaxing. However, I have found a few brilliant tricks and tips that I always offer to other dyslexic people: simple but very specific ideas such as spacing of sentences, certain fonts, the colour of paper and visual punctuation are an absolute must.

When I see words, I instantly tense up, my heart rate rises; I feel like I sweat a lot when I start looking at the page, I feel rushed. I feel like I have to be absolutely on my guard when I'm reading, especially when I am reading aloud. When I see words, they frighten me, and that is such a shame – I actually wish I loved words, but it's all about perception. It is a constant battle, and it never eases up, it never gets easier. In light of that, I have this weird love–hate relationship with words. I also have a never-ending challenge to find a way to love words. Yet I know with words that I will never get a perfect ten.

You can see now that I am the world's biggest 'try hard', right, so I will keep going at something until I can achieve it. When I look back at all the random paths my life has taken – from the foundation of farming to gymnastics, theatre, juggling, unicycling, TV presenting, charity marathons, art, production . . . and many more unexpected twists and turns – it makes me smile at how varied, fascinating and hugely enjoyable it has all been. People often see someone doing something exciting or successful and dismiss that by saying, 'Oh, he's really lucky,' but you can only do that if you are ready for that new direction. I have always worked really hard to try to succeed – as I've said, gymnastics taught me that, all those years ago: if you graft and graft then you will get a result. If you don't try your hardest then it just doesn't happen, simple as that.

So many things pass you by, unless you are ready for them with your experience and your skills. If you are ready for those moments and are able to react when they present themselves, then it is amazing what direction your life can go. Part of the excitement is that you never know when you might need your skills.

In my opinion, anybody who is reading this can do anything. You have just got to work really hard to make it happen. When you find your way of doing something, you work rock hard and don't stop until you are satisfied. Then you move on and find something else to work hard at.

You could sum up my view on life with an old saying I've always lived by: 'Luck is a lifetime of preparation for a moment of opportunity.'

So, bearing all this in mind, how does my dyslexia make me feel? Well, in all honesty, when I'm not around words it makes me feel really confident that I can see things that other people can't. It makes me feel that I notice things differently and *I like that*. It gives me that ability to have a photographic memory because I *see* things and remember them in a visual way. I live in a world of imagery and that feels pretty empowering. When you have dyslexia, you become very good at figuring out ways around challenges. You find a way to achieve something or get around a problem using your wits. It really enables you to think on your feet.

I would go further than that and actually say that I love the fact that I'm dyslexic. I can't speak highly enough of what it's given me – this different perspective on life, the fact that I don't do things the same way as other people. If you asked me if I could do it all again and not be dyslexic, I would say, 'No, thanks.' That's because I wouldn't want to do it without the perspective of life that I have, that dyslexia has given to me.

Dyslexia obviously impacts my life, every day, but in my mind, as many people feel, being dyslexic is a superpower.

Reflecting on the topic of being in tune with nature, I want to go back to my love of art. Of course, with my gymnastics, then college and zooming off into *Blue Peter* and the world of TV, my art has often got sidelined. I never forgot it, but it just became quite hard to find the time. Then, a few years ago, I started to paint again, and the second I did, I felt this over-whelming sense of contentment, of being in tune with my surroundings.

And where better to escape and paint or draw than our farm?

The tones of the farm are just sensational. The warm tones of autumn, all the golden hues, the fresh greens and vibrancy of spring, the barren whites and darks of winter and, of course, summer in all its multicoloured glory. It's hard NOT to enjoy painting when you're surrounded by a constant stream of inspiring visuals.

I remember going with *Countryfile* to where John Constable painted 'The Hay Wain' back around 1821. That extremely famous painting depicts a rural scene on the River Stour, not far from Flatford Mill in Suffolk. There are three horses pulling a wooden wain (a type of wagon) across the water and that work is widely regarded as one of the greatest of all English works of art. Luckily for me, *Countryfile* has been a rich source of material for my art. I often take photos on my phone of what I liked during the day and then frequently start sketching away in the car on the way home. Travelling was also a fantastic opportunity for my art – I painted in the Atlas Mountains, in Monterey Bay, all over the world. When I was in Monterey Bay, I had a rare day off and went and found an art shop, then bought a little pack of watercolours and some brushes and art paper. Then I had the most delightful time, sitting on some rocks by the water, just painting the beautiful seascape.

That idea, of painting a landscape that you are a part of, is incredibly compelling to me. It goes back to what I was saying about being a part of your surroundings. It is about noticing stuff, appreciating all the tiny details and revelling in that richness. I'm in a different state of mind when I start sketching or painting. The whole process takes me away from the pressures of work and the pace of its demands; you set up, start to examine the landscape, make a few decisions, sketch some ideas, and focus on what is there in front of you and how it makes you feel, as against what's in, or on, your mind.

My style isn't to try to recreate a landscape exactly the same as real life – if you want to do that, take a photograph. It is of course entirely subjective, but I prefer to create my interpretation of what I have been looking at, and what it conjures up. I survey the view and mull over how I want to portray that on canvas – sometimes it is quite literal, sometimes it ends up being almost surreal. Whatever takes my fancy on that day, to be honest. I also use many different mediums: watercolour, acrylic or oil. I don't know what it's going to look like when I start out but that is part of the excitement and reward.

My greatest family holidays have always had art at their heart. My dream of going to Disney World came true when Mum and Dad surprised us with tickets to Florida under the placemats of our Christmas dinner one year. I couldn't believe we were going to the home of my childhood sketching inspiration. I wasn't as excited about the rides as I was about the fact I was going to meet those artists and watch them draw.

Another massive inspiration was Saint-Paul de Vence in France. My friend Gloria Hunniford, who I'd known for years due to our *Blue Peter* connection, invited us to stay in her villa in the south of France one summer. My whole family went out there with me, my mum, my dad, my mother-in-law, Nicola and the kids . . . While we were there, we took a trip to visit Saint-Paul de Vence, where all the great masters such as Picasso, Matisse and Chagall used to paint. The old town is full of galleries and art museums, so I was in my element. Wandering around the cobbled streets soaking up the same environment as those great artists . . . I loved it, and talk about inspirational for my art. There was a certain time of day when the sunlight would drop down and the scenes around you just began to emerge . . . it was an amazing place to do art. I spent most of the holiday painting!

On one trip for *Countryfile*, we were working down in Kimmeridge Bay on the Jurassic Coast, filming a local artist. I was given some fossilized squid ink that had been ground up and mixed with seawater, in order to paint an artist's impression on some water-colour paper of what the squid would've looked like, using its own ink. I didn't finish it that day but brought the ink back in a little bottle, so I could finish the picture at home – Nicola has that up in her office now.

Whenever we are in a hotel, I take ages getting to my room or down to breakfast because I love spending time looking at all the art on the walls. I particularly love the small, regional hotels or B & Bs that we often use for filming – they will usually have local art on the walls. Sometimes it is a mini-exhibition and you can almost always buy these pictures for a very reasonable price. I can stand there for ages, just looking. I will often ask the owner who the artist is and try to find out their back story, too. It's so important to actually LOOK at a painting, stand in front of it and learn from the artist's choices. Give it a try next time . . . instead of rushing past.

If you have wondered about art, I would urge you to just have a go. As children we love to paint, don't we? No inhibitions, we just dive in and get paint all over our hands and slap it everywhere and have a great time – well, why should that change in adult-hood? At first, what you see on the page or canvas will probably not reflect what you had in your mind, but that's not important. It's all about trying, practising, improving and, before long, you will be creating your own style and, I guarantee you, art will become an interesting addition to your life.

Before I started on social media, nobody knew I painted. I'd never put any of my art out there. A few friends urged me to post some examples of my art on Instagram but I was very apprehensive – it's so personal, you know? Eventually I did – memorably, I was sitting in my dressing room at the London Palladium (I was in panto there), and I was looking at a photo I'd sent to Mum and Dad, of an oil painting I'd done of a landscape of a lake with late-autumnal trees. For some reason, I made the decision to go for it and do a post! And I was taken aback by the reaction: people seemed to really like it and were keen to interact and show me the artists in their own families.

I think that maybe my visual interpretation of life, fuelled by my dyslexia, might also be why I find making TV programmes so rewarding. I love film, I love photography, I just can't get enough of anything visual that is emotive and striking.

Like art – but most definitely not like modern life – farming and the countryside need masses of patience. Many things that farmers do are VERY slow. Sure, they have delivery deadlines and lots of commercial pressures, but a crop doesn't sprout overnight, a sheep might not be ready to breed for two years, a hedgerow won't be mature for many years, an orchard might not mature for a decade. The list is endless. However, I love that slower pace. I love the fact it all takes time – I find that very grounding.

And the learning itself can't be rushed; the skills are passed on by older generations, then you can add to them through personal experience, but that all takes time. I think if you spend enough time outdoors, that patience builds up inside.

Life doesn't need to be a perpetual state of rushing around.

If you spend more time in nature, you will appreciate its beauty more every time and you will also feel the losses more keenly – by that I mean, if you are unaware of something, then you won't notice when it's gone. Imagine an animal that you know nothing about . . . and it becomes extinct before you see it. It's gone but that makes no impact on your life whatsoever. If you didn't know it existed to start with, it is not a loss to you. That's not ignorance, that's not a criticism of people, it's just a suggestion to try to spend as much time getting to know your surroundings as you possibly can, because it is a win–win for you and our countryside.

As I have got older, I have found myself increasingly reflective and I really enjoy these more contemplative moments. When I was a young lad, with all my sport and going off on all my travels, there was a real excitement in and taste for adventure, a real drive for achievement. On reflection, I think that you get to the age where I am now and you start to think, *Actually, I've been off there, I've done all these amazing things, from the Amazon to the Arctic Circle, to meeting royalty, pop stars, travelling the world, I've met loads of people and filled three passports with experiences. But right now, I'd love to go and put up that owl box.*

Everything was so fast paced when I was younger, and I never really stopped to think about all those incredible experiences. You don't need to have been as fortunate as I have with my globe-trotting times – just pausing for a moment to listen, look and sense nature seems to help people take time out and contemplate what they have achieved.

Modern life is so scheduled and controlled and, let's face it, *rushed*, you've got to have a plan of action, schedules, meetings, diary dates, everything is regimented and, if you're not careful, you kind of just jump on board the ride and tick the boxes and get taken along without really ever being in charge of your own time.

Partly as a consequence of this hectic nature of modern life, I think that, unfortunately, a lot of people have lost sight of the notion of being in tune with wildlife and the countryside. If I've had a full-on day and I'm stressed when I come back home, I just have to stand here and listen and think about the stresses that wildlife goes through every second of every day. Everything is out there trying to feed, trying to build a home, trying to survive. Trying not to get eaten! I really respect the struggles that the natural world goes through, too. That's not to belittle any of our struggles, because sadly many people are faced with terrible challenges each day. But if you are able to find a path out to the countryside, a field, a hilly walk or a peaceful valley, just any natural environment, if you can find time to immerse yourself in all of that . . . it *will* enrich your life.

11

# A Lifetime's Passion

One of the biggest challenges – perhaps THE biggest challenge – for our farm is that we are 100 per cent organic. Organic produce is often significantly more expensive than non-organic. That's just a fact. It is also a fact that many people are simply not in a position to spend the money on organic food.

Back in the day, Mum started to think about going organic when people thought the idea was a bit 'hippyish' or 'out there'. There were very few farmers set up to help her become organic and she had to do an enormous amount of research on her own.

At the time of writing, there are far more organic farms than back then, but they still represent a very tiny percentage of the UK's agricultural capacity. According to figures published by DEFRA, in 2019 the United Kingdom had a total area of 485,000 hectares of land farmed organically. This represents 2.7 per cent of the total farmed area on agricultural holdings in the United Kingdom, and 63 per cent of organic farmland is permanent grassland.

Our land has been organically farmed for well over twenty years. The set-up of our farm really lent itself to the organic way, being a hill farm. Also, Mum loved the animal side a lot more than the machinery or crop elements. With the woodland and the type of grazing we have, it was a simple but steady transition. We try to maintain a healthy natural system of working with nature, from the soil to the plants and then the animals. There are many much, MUCH bigger farms in the UK than our hundred acres. Some of the biggest are over ten thousand acres. Mostly they will be non-organic, simply due to the sheer scale and requirements of operating on that massive level. For us, we can be more flexible and nimble, although with it mainly being my parents, with assistance from

Nicola and myself, and friends who come to help out, farming a hundred acres organically remains a tricky balance.

In the UK, our agricultural framework – the rules and regulations – are considered by many to be *the most stringent in the world* for both organic and non-organic. The regulations are so strict, so exacting and so tightly policed that there are innumerable hoops for all farmers to jump through every day. And that is something of which we should be VERY proud of our farmers for. It's definitely not easy but it should be shouted from the rooftops that our farmers have such high standards. It's not always easy, but it is fantastic that standards are SO high.

When it comes to organic farming, the rules are tighter still. Take grass as a simple example: the authorities are very strict about when you cut your grass, how much you can cut your grass, what you can put on your land, when you can do it, even to within a certain month.

There are extremely strict guidelines about fertilizers and pesticides. There are prescribed lists of what is acceptable and what is not. We 'top' the grazed fields with a topper mower (a giant lawn mower raised up that just takes the 'tops' off) just over the invasive weeds such as thistles and docks, rather than using pesticides. Nettles are a 'good weed' in our eyes so they get left for the caterpillars, aphids and lady-birds.

Maintenance and enhancement of soil life and natural soil fertility, soil stability and soil biodiversity are the main principles on which everything else is based on our farm. The use of fertilizers, pesticides and medicines that all end up in, or on, the soil, affect nature's delicate balance. Taking soil samples is a good tool, to discover what plant life is growing, but also to track the health of the soil. Our samples show we have a shortage of selenium on our land, so it's agreed that we put out mineral blocks all year round which contain extra selenium. The sheep take it as and when they want.

Also, the use of medicine can be an added complication for an organic farmer, whose focus has to be on boosting more natural immunity rather than relying on medication; that said, the rule is always that the welfare of the animal comes first, so in certain circumstances, permission is granted.

We have a health plan for the animals which is reviewed by the organic body during our 'on-farm annual inspection'. We can discuss any issues we have had with the sheep, be it bad feet or blow fly, worms, etc., and make sure the medication we use, if and when required, is the correct one. We also work with our vet if there is anything out of the ordinary that we need to use at any point in the year, and we can ask permission from our organic body to do so.

A truly organic farm has to be so low impact that stocking it heavily with large numbers of livestock just isn't feasible or allowed.

We try and make best use of the natural resources we have. Once the polytunnel is mucked out after lambing, we spread the muck produced in there on the land at the end of the year, which helps put nutrients back into the land, but only at a time when a layer of muck won't damage or smother the meadow.

All of the UK's regulations are incredibly particular and, inevitably, adhering to them costs money. Organic farming is most definitely not a quick route to an easy buck. You have to be prepared to be proactive, to work with a focus on prevention more than cure. You have to predict when something is going to happen, rather than react after it does.

As I mentioned, our farm is modest by comparison to some modern farms. Back in the day, if we had run this as a mixed farm – namely arable and livestock – then you could've scraped something of a living from this place. However, running it as an organic livestock farm is pretty limiting in terms of its commercial potential. You'd need at least double the acreage to make it work, plus even then you'd need to farm it more intensively than we do. These days, in competition with all of those supermarket suppliers and commercial elements like that, a hundred acres is nothing.

This is a core dilemma moving forward with a population that is growing fast: how do we feed that nation, at the same time as doing what's best for the landscape and its wildlife residents that we all love? If our population is going to continually increase, how can we sustainably feed all those new mouths?

Modern farming is an intense and demanding lifestyle. You've got all the demands of feeding, the pressures of agriculture, the weather, the competition with supermarkets, milk, wool and meat prices, legislation, regulation, export issues – there is a whole book's worth of challenges, all of which can be so difficult to deal with as a farmer.

The challenge for British farmers right across the board is to somehow work around 'the supermarket disconnect'. That consumer standing there, financially pressured maybe, lots to do, kids to sort out, jobs to get done, they have one choice of food in each hand and the decision which to buy is driven by price. We need to inform people about WHY the quality of one product means it is more expensive, explain the details, the restrictions, and the reasons why different farming practices across the world create different prices.

What I would say is, whatever you choose to eat, at least take some time to find out that the quality of that product is the very best you can afford.

In my opinion, in this country those standards that are written down in law are without doubt the best in the world. We have – also without doubt – the best farmers in the world, too.

So when our UK products are more expensive than those of another country where none of those standards are required . . . well, you have to make a decision as a consumer. I am, of course, making the assumption that you can afford to choose – if you are lucky enough to have a choice about what you put on your plate, just ask yourself a couple of simple questions:

*Where does the quality of the food I buy sit on my priority list?*

*Why is this food so cheap?*

I think farming is a compulsion, a way of life; it pulls on you from deep inside and you can't control that or snuff it out. It is part of you. I feel very lucky that the work we do on our farm will be passed to later generations and resonate for many centuries. The

British landscape right across the UK looks the way it does because of the way the land has been tended. Everywhere you look, farmers have made a difference. People rightly talk about 'the beautiful British countryside', but actually there are only very modest amounts that are truly wild, even to the point where many of those have been 'allowed' to go wild. British farmers are the reason that this country looks the way it does, they are the reason why millions of people flock here and why it's world-renowned. That is due to centuries of work, of care, of expertise. On our farm in the Dales, we are planting the building blocks for the future. Implementing all these ideas will only create a more efficient, enjoyable farm to live on. Luke and Molly and all the young members of our wider family will enjoy the benefits of that, because by the time they could live here and work the farm, the ideas that we've implemented will have been in place for years. I have never forced my kids to do anything that they didn't want to do; as a parent, I think it is our job to introduce our children to as many different things as possible and let them decide. I know how good the farming life has been for me, and I am delighted to say that they seem to love it, too.

The aim is that the next generation has the choice to inherit a farm that sits well in its surroundings.

That is why I feel like I am a part of that legacy of generations of farmers, and it feels like a real blessing to say that.

I honestly believe that.

I love this way of life, I know these people and, certainly in my experience, our farmers are passionate, hard-working, skilled custodians.

No farmer doesn't love the land – no farmer.

And, as a nation, we are lucky to have them.

# Epilogue: 'That'll Do'

I feel incredibly privileged that I was brought up on a farm, in a countryside community and with wildlife and Mother Nature as constant companions throughout my life.

Having read this book, I hope that you maybe feel inclined to be out there amid the fields and hills, the valleys and hedgerows, to see, hear, smell and just sense this world we live in. I understand that it is not so easy for everyone to enjoy nature and the countryside, but you don't need to own your own farm to get stuck in and involved – there are loads of volunteer schemes that you can join. These armies of volunteers do so much of the good work that keeps our countryside healthy and so diverse. We have a great relationship with the Wildlife Trust and there are other organizations you can get involved with, too.

If you make the effort to immerse yourself in nature and our breathtaking countryside, you will feel great – your health will benefit.

When I went down to London to audition for *Blue*

*Peter*, I was content in the knowledge that if it didn't work out, then my worst-case scenario was my best-case scenario – I'd come back to the farm. Among all the chatter and noise of modern life, for me there is no better feeling than getting up, working a hard day out on the farm, then coming back in to sit by the fire, eat some food, and go to bed, exhausted but happy. To this day, I get invited to quite a few 'celebrity' parties, whatever that means, but I'd sooner be up on the hill with my dog or painting a picture or walking around the woods or lambing the sheep.

That feeling has followed me all my life, the idea that no matter how things away from the farm pan out, it is always there for me: the animals, the fields, the woodland, the valley, our farmhouse. I can't lose. That fact has encouraged me to take risks with my career but also to have no fear or trepidation when it seems like time to walk away from something.

I've travelled the world and I know that if being back here, on our farm, is my worst-case scenario . . . then that'll do.

# Tour of the Farm

Let me take you on a little tour of our farm which, as you know, is nestled in the middle of nowhere in a beautiful valley. You turn off the main road and drive along a very lengthy farm track that is three-quarters of a mile long. You eventually turn the corner at the bottom, then head up to the farmhouse at the top of the steep hill, perched on the side of a valley – it is sitting there, as it has since the 1600s. It is an old-school farmhouse with a byre to the left-hand side and a stable block to the left of that, which then leads round to a centrally enclosed courtyard in the middle. All the beautiful old sandstone buildings have had various bits of work done to them over many years, some have been reroofed and other parts have been rebuilt over generations. They're all part of the farm's story.

Another track goes all the way around the farmhouse and outbuildings before scooping down towards another road that leads off towards our hay shed, sheep pens and polytunnel, situated next to a line of tall trees that act as a windbreak from the west winds, which can be pretty savage. We have four paddocks that are directly in front of the farmhouse itself, so we can keep a close eye on anything we pop in there, as we look out of the house.

At the bottom of the valley is our ancient woodland. We have four sections of ancient woodlands: the top two sections are fenced for grazing and are more open; the lower sections drop down right into the valley bottom – those are much denser woodlands.

To the right-hand side of those woodlands are two fields – the top and bottom woodland hay meadows. The 'gath' – a grassed and hedge-lined alleyway – leads up to the flat road field which comes back along the farm track. Opposite this field on the other side of our track is another hay meadow that we call our top hay field. Over on the other side of the farm, we have our two big hill fields, the top one that stretches the full height from the hill all the way down the valley, and then also a bottom hill field which goes right up to the ancient woodland. The donkeys have their own section to the side of the farmhouse, complete with miniature stables and two donkey paddocks. The goats also have a paddock just for them, which backs on to our orchard in the old hill garden.

I love nothing more than driving up the track, closing the gate and indulging in all these sections of the farm; over the course of my lifetime I have come to know them so well . . . every nook and cranny.

# Sources

There are so many incredible websites offering very expert information on every element of wildlife that you can think of. I have referenced a few below that were useful in collating this book, and hopefully they will get you started on learning more!

**Ancient Woodland:**
woodlandtrust.org.uk/trees-woods-and-wildlife/habitats/ancient-woodland/

**Barn Owls:**
barnowltrust.org.uk/barn-owl-facts/

rspb.org.uk/birds-and-wildlife/bird-and-wildlife-guides/ask-an-expert/previous/barnowlfeathers.aspx

**Bats:**
bats.org.uk

**Black Welsh Mountain Sheep:**
blackwelshmountain.org.uk

**Butterflies:**
stnicks.org.uk

**Cheviots:**
cheviotsheep.org

**Chickens:**
www.thehappychickencoop.com

**Coal Mining:**
durhamrecordoffice.org.uk/article/10560/Coal-Mining-and-Durham-Collieries

**Drystone Walls:**
bbc.co.uk/news/av/magazine-33819675

britainexpress.com/History/drystone.htm

nationalstonecentre.org.uk

**Fordson Tractors:**
ssbtractor.com/features/Ford_tractors.html

**Hampshires:**
hampshiredown.org.uk

https://www.mad-farmer.co.uk/hampshire%20down.html

**Hebrideans:**
hebrideansheep.org.uk

**Herdwicks:**
herdy.co.uk

**Hualapai Native Americans:**
hualapai-nsn.gov/about-2/

**Insects:**
rspb.org.uk

**Lambing:**
countrysideonline.co.uk/food-and-farming/
feeding-the-nation/livestock/british-lambing-
season/

nationalsheep.org.uk/uk-sheep-industry/sheep-in-
the-uk/the-sheep-farming-year/

**Mashams:**
www.masham-sheep.co.uk

**Pheasants:**
pheasantsforever.org/Habitat/Pheasant-Facts.aspx

**Rickshaw:**
express.co.uk/life-style/health/283692/Matt-Baker-
I-m-back-in-the-saddle

**Shearing:**
bbc.co.uk/news/uk-england-cornwall-36895648

toa.st/blogs/magazine/a-brief-history-of-sheep-
shearing

**Sheep/Sheep Farming:**
Culture and Nature: The European Heritage of
Sheep Farming and Pastoral Life.

Introduction and History of Sheep Farming in
the UK. Research Report for the UK by Simon

Bell and Gemma Bell, Estonian University of Life Sciences November 2011

culturalecology.info/pastoralism/thoughtData/47/Hisory%20sheep%20farming%20uk.pdf

**Shetlands:**
*Horse & Hound* magazine www.horseandhound.co.uk/features/shetland-pony-facts-673878

**Starling Murmurations:**
lancswt.org.uk/blog/charlotte-varela/starling-murmuration-facts

livinglevels.org.uk/stories/2019/1/26/starling-murmurations

**Tree Sparrows:** rspb.org.uk/birds-and-wildlife/wildlife-guides/bird-a-z/tree-sparrow/

# Acknowledgements

I mention in the book how some people have a fleeting chapter in your life but are incredibly influential, so I'd like to thank everyone that's helped me get to where I am.

It goes without saying I owe a huge amount to my family; they are my inspiration and why I do what I do.

I'd like to thank Dan Bunyard, Aggie Russell, Bea McIntyre and the whole team at Michael Joseph for making this book a reality. Thanks also to Martin Roach for helping me tell my story. I've thoroughly enjoyed my first venture into the world of books.